M000111559

1

The Financial Guide to Retiring Abroad

How to retire overseas, avoid tax, invest wisely, and save your money

By Rick Todd

Commonsensical Publishing, Los Angeles, California, USA

www.expatinvesting.org

Copyright © 2011 by Rick Todd

ISBN 978-1-4507-3560-5

Do not copy or republish this book without express permission from the author. Individuals who copy this book without permission of the author are in violation of U.S. Copyright Law and if caught will be prosecuted to the fullest extent possible.

Table of Contents

OVERVIEW

Anyone who tells you that retiring abroad is easy, that you can buy super-cheap properties hassle free right on the beach, or that there are plenty of places where the locals love foreigners and the food is great is **a liar**. Retiring abroad is one of the most difficult things you can do, but if done properly, can be one of the most **rewarding** things you can do. There are enormous obstacles to overcome. You will need to immerse yourself in the local culture, you will need to have an in-depth understanding of how the local government works (and perhaps how to avoid it), and most importantly you will need to have an understanding of the **financial aspects of retirement**. My goal with this book is give you the best preparation possible for what can either be the **best years of your life**, or a period of misery and **poverty**.

A definition of retirement

Books about retirement are never really clear in defining exactly what retirement is. In my opinion retirement is defined as a period of time when an individual has largely ceased working and lives off an income from pensions (both public and private sector) and savings withdrawals. Day to day work has ceased, at least for pay.

In order to successfully retire, and by successfully retire I mean to have a **high enough income to live relatively well** without working, you must have saved a considerable amount of money in your career. With the average person retiring in their mid- to late- 60s, but going on to live as long as two decades after their retirement, an essential part of your retirement plan must involve finances. Bizarrely, most retirement guides gloss over this key element of retirement. If they talk about retiring abroad they simply describe the various cultural and geographic elements of whatever destination they are currently writing about. While those are certainly important (I like to know where the good restaurants are, too), they are nowhere near as important as having the financial knowledge that will enable you to afford to live the good life.

Why you should read this book

One of the purposes of this book is to make you think long and hard about all the difficulties as well as the advantages of living and retiring abroad. Most books and websites that advocate retiring abroad paint a **rosy picture** of what you'll have to look forward to. They'll recommend that you buy property, preferably from one of the real estate agents they recommend (usually for a kickback) and they'll extol the virtues of whatever country you've chosen.

The most popular reason why people move abroad

The biggest reason people pack up and move to a new and strange country and leave their friends and family behind is because the new country is **less expensive to live in**. The cost of food is less, the cost of housing is less, the cost of having a housekeeper is less. However, the popular axiom that **you get what you pay for** comes into play. The quality of housing might be less than what you are used to, the food isn't that great, and the labor you hire is incompetent compared to the labor you hired back home. In addition to all that, you may strive for a lifestyle that is extremely expensive in the country you move to. That flat screen TV, that giant washer and dryer set, all cost **more than what you would pay for them at home**. You neglected to realize that the country you moved to had higher tariffs on imported goods, and that the reality of day-to-day life was very different from your previous vacation stays.

Yes, the reality is different

Moving and living abroad is very difficult. It is even more difficult if you don't speak the **local language**. If you decide to move to the developing world, like Latin America or Southeast Asia, **poverty** will be rife. Coming from the first world to the third world is a trip back in time in many respects. You will be entering countries where the role of women is still in flux. You will not have access to the wide variety of luxuries you took for granted. You will find that the country you moved to, though poorer, is not actually **cheaper**. In many ways it might even be more expensive!

Reasons for moving abroad

While much of this book may read like a **Donnie Downer**, there are many reasons why you should consider retiring abroad. Moving and living in a foreign country is an experience like no other. It gives you a sense of freedom unlike any you can possibly have, both in a financial sense and in a legal sense. You will experience different cultures, customs, cuisines, and imagery that are entirely new. This book is an attempt to help you gain these new and exciting experiences.

Money is the biggest key to your success

There is an enormous misconception about moving abroad. Typically a person who is about to retire is thinking about moving abroad because he or she feels that the cost of living in their current country is too high. This person assumes, usually incorrectly, that they will be able to maintain their standard of living, and even improve it, for far less money than they currently spend.

Anyone who tells you that is selling you a **pipe dream**. Yes, it is very possible to live well and to live on far less than you currently live on in the developed world. However, if you think you will be able to live in a giant villa with an army of servants on the beach, think again. Rentals are typically somewhat cheaper, but property can be just as expensive. I will go over the substantial risks in buying property, and the cost of living in various popular retirement destinations around the world. The subject is far more complex than you imagined.

Taxes and their crucial importance

For some odd reason most books that discuss retiring abroad gloss over taxes and the issues related to them. Taxes should be at the forefront of your decision to move to a given country. In this book I will look at the various **tax havens** throughout the world and how moving to them should be a key consideration. If you are an American you are required by law to continue to pay taxes **even if you live abroad**. Also, depending on the state where you formerly lived, you may even owe state income tax.

The United States is one of the few countries that continues to tax its citizens no matter where they live. As bad as this seems, there are still considerable tax benefits for an American living abroad **as long as you choose to live in a country that is tax-friendly to foreigners.** Other Westerners can avoid taxes altogether, but this only kicks in if they live in their new country for a certain period of time, and over the course of most of the year. These are things that are rarely mentioned in other retirement guides, and if they are, they are only glossed over.

How to retire in the first place

While books of all kinds tell you where to retire, they don't tell you **how to get there.** In this book I will devote an entire chapter to actually saving for retirement and give you reading recommendations as well as an overview on the best investments to have. I will also tell you the best investments to **avoid.** I have never seen a book that discusses retiring abroad talk about actually how to retire in the first place. These books **assume** that you already have thousands if not millions of Dollars/Pounds/Euros squirreled away. I do not make that assumption.

The good news about learning to save for retirement is that the key things to invest are available to anyone in the world. That means that the investment advice I will give is relevant to anyone in the world. What do I advocate investing in? I'll give you a hint: they're called index funds (tracking funds in Europe).

Non-political

A growing trend in books on moving abroad is to get into the politics of it. Not in this book! I couldn't **care less** if you are a left- winger who chaffs against authoritarian government and wants to go native and live free of worry in the jungles of India or South America. I also couldn't care less if you are a right-winger who feels **oppressed** by excessive taxation in your home country and seeks to live in a mansion tax-free with hundreds of servants. I simply want to give you the best possible guide to living well abroad and getting the experience you've always dreamed of.

Throughout this book, I have made every effort to be as unbiased and apolitical as possible. The various ways I give you to avoid wasting money are not in any way an effort to help you hurt governments and locals, but rather legal means to not get hurt yourself. I've lived poor in foreign countries, and I've lived well in foreign countries, and I can assure you, living well in foreign countries far outweighs living poor (unless you're into that type of thing).

Why my book is different

When I sell you my book that is all I am selling you. Many other websites will try to sell you property and other extremely risky investments. I have no interest in anything other than giving you reasonable advice based on my years of living abroad, my legal background, and my extensive travel history. I am not associated with anyone else, or any other company. I am simply making use of extensive research and common sense to give you the best possible guide to **surviving and thriving** abroad.

You will see in the next chapters how important it is that you adequately prepare for life in another country. I will endeavor to make you think long and hard as to whether it is the right choice for you, and whether you could be picking a more "boring" country to live in rather than some more exotic locale.

This book emphasizes the financial aspects of moving abroad for two reasons. One, I feel it is usually overlooked in retirement guides or glossed over. Typically financial discussions concern personal budgeting and coupon-clipping. While those are certainly important, they reveal that the author either has no real understanding of personal finance or simply doesn't care. The second reason I feel personal finance should be emphasized is that it is so important. You simply cannot do anything without money. Having the money necessary to live well is just as important as eating well and getting exercise. However, **this is not a book on how to become rich**. I am not rich, and have no clue on how to get rich. I am middle-class and live comfortably, and that is the sort of knowledge I will try to instill. There are thousands of books written on how to get rich, and almost all of them written by con artists and sociopaths who would love to steal your money. I advise you to avoid them.

Reasons for NOT moving abroad

While most travel and retirement guides will describe the wonders of moving abroad, few if any like to challenge the reader with reasons why you should **not** move abroad. Before you decide to make the trip overseas permanent, take some time to think over the potential challenges and difficulties you might face. A brief list should suffice to act as a reasonable wake-up call to the endless possibilities of problems and strife that can occur in living abroad:

- Traffic is out of control and extremely dangerous (a significant problem in the developing world)
- Hygiene of locals is suspect
- Weather, while normally idyllic, is occasionally severe (hurricanes, earthquakes etc.)
- Hospitals and healthcare are subpar compared to home
- Crime is rampant
- Poverty is rampant
- Communicating with locals is difficult
- Customs are so different that one is uncomfortable
- Local cuisine is upsetting

- Special dietary needs are not easily met (vegetarian, diabetic, kosher, halal etc.)
- Businesses and residences are not handicap-accessible
- You face lack of contact with friends and family back home

Obviously these problems are magnified when you take into consideration the age and health of the typical retiree. Living abroad is fraught with dangers, some of which may be more abundant than in the retiree's home country. Think carefully before proceeding.

Definitions

Throughout this book I will use the terms "Westerner", "developed", "developing", "third world", and "first world". These are important terms and it is essential that you know their definitions. Forgive me if you already do, and simply skip this section.

The terms "first world" and "developed" are interchangeable, with the former term being considered old fashioned and the latter term more modern. They refer to the parts of the world where people live well and have easy access to modern technology. This part of the world includes the United States and Canada, Australia and New Zealand, Western Europe and the nations within it, Japan, Singapore, Hong Kong, and by some definitions South Korea, Taiwan, and Israel. You might also include the parts of the world that are either closely associated with, or entirely governed by the United States or Western European powers like France and the United Kingdom. Examples of these would be Barbados, the Cayman Islands, the Virgin Islands (both British and American), New Caledonia, Tahiti etc. These areas are almost always islands, and often run their economies on a mixture of tourism and offshore financial services. More on these later.

Overview

As you might have guessed, the remainder of the world is "developing" or the "third world". Just because a country is not in the developed world does not mean that it is poor. On the contrary: in the Persian Gulf area the country with the highest per capita income in the world is Qatar. However, no one would consider that nation to be developed. Being developed does not only mean being relatively wealthy. It also means having **transparent laws**, a democratic system of government, a diverse economy, and a fair legal system. The vast majority of countries that are seen as developing are either poor, unfair to many to the people who reside within their borders, or both.

Many of the recommendations I make in this book will refer to the developing world, rather than the developed world. The differences between the developing world and the developed world are so great that an **extensive discussion** needs to occur in order for you to be prepared to successfully retire there. If a recommendation I make is valid in any country, including the developed world, I'll make note of it.

Why are these definitions important? For many retirees who wish to retire abroad, the most common journey is from the developed world to the developing world, particularly if you are an American or Canadian. For many Europeans, retiring abroad is something that Northern Europeans do when they move to other nations within the European Union. According to a survey conducted by the BBC in 2006, the most popular destinations for British pensioners were the following countries in order of popularity:

1. Australia (245,000)
2. Canada (157,000)
3. United States (132,000)
4. Spain (74,000)
5. New Zealand (47,000)

6. South Africa (39,000)
7. Italy (34,000)
8. France (34,000)
9. Germany (33,000)
10. Cyprus (12,000)
11. Portugal (6,000)

Many of those destinations were chosen to take advantage of a lower cost of living, better weather, and a better and less crowded lifestyle. Americans are no different: according to the Association of Americans Overseas, **5.25 million** Americans live abroad (excluding military personnel). In Latin America and Canada there are 2.2 million, in Europe 1.4 million, and in East Asia and Oceania 754,000. For their own bizarre reasons, the U.S. State Department and the Census do not keep accurate information about the exact number of Americans abroad but the numbers above show that there is a significant number of Westerners who are moving abroad for work opportunities and, more importantly, to enjoy a **cheaper and better lifestyle**. Many of those overseas are retirees who seek to live out the rest of their days in their own versions of paradise. As the Western world ages demographically, it is important that we look at the incentives to move and the benefits of moving abroad.

Demographic shift and an incentive to move

All around the world we are seeing fewer and fewer children being born and the population in general growing older. With the world's population moving into cities and away from rural areas, the incentive for families to have many children has declined considerably.

In the developed world, the issue is considerably magnified. According to the United States Census Bureau, the number of people aged over 65 will increase from a little over 40 million people in 2010 to 55 million in 2020, with 6.6 million people within that group aged 85 or older. By 2040 America will be home to approximately 81 million people over the age of 65, with 14 million people in that group aged 85 or older. That many millions of elderly people will require substantial numbers of younger people to take care of their needs as they age and grow infirm.

This is not a problem limited to the United States. The entire developed world is growing older. In Italy in the year 2000, 18 per cent of Italians were over the age of 65. In Greece, Sweden, Japan and Spain, over 17 per cent of the population was over 65. The aging of the developed world is quickly and quietly reaching crisis proportions. Europe is currently the "oldest" part of the world and according to the Census, by 2050 29 per cent of its population will be 65 or older.

With such a profound need for assisted living caretakers you can bet that the price of labor will rise sharply. Without enough young people to do the necessary work to take care of so many elderly people, the only way to prevent labor from growing too expensive will be to allow for unprecedented immigration. If the country you live in is in any way xenophobic, this could be an enormous problem for you as you grow old and require care.

The demographics of the developing world are somewhat different. Populations there are far younger, and that means they will be an even greater source of cheap labor than they are now. As a retiree abroad you may be able to take advantage of that. Labor at the source is far cheaper than labor imported from far away. But be aware that while you might be taking advantage of cheap labor, you are also dealing with labor that will be far less professional and hard-working than immigrant labor. In other words, **you get what you pay for**.

The Westerner abroad

This book's primary audience is **Westerners**. I define a Westerner as a person who has spent most of his or her life in a developed country. Westerner is no longer a racial classification as the countries that make up the West are diverse, and in some cases, no longer even located in the Western part of the globe. Also, Westerners are always citizens of these countries. This is an important point, as having a **Western passport** is a very important tool that will help you successfully settle in another country in retirement. Sadly, the world is divided into a giant class system, and those with passports from the developed world are given a great deal of access to developing countries, while those with only developing world passports are given highly restricted if any access at all to the developed world.

As a Westerner, you carry a passport that is a source of immense power and prestige. It can be a legal defense that gives you far more rights than the average citizen of the country you wish to move to. But it can also make you a target for crime and considerable scrutiny. When you travel and retire to a poorer part of the world as a Westerner you will be seen as someone with **more wealth** than most (even if that is not really the case), and you will be seen as someone who is **more professional and better educated** than most (again, even if that is not the case). Behave accordingly.

The dream can be a reality

You have purchased this book because you want information that will get help you move abroad and live the retirement you've always dreamed about. If you want to experience the beautiful beaches of Cancún on a daily basis, if you want to live in an apartment overlooking Rio de la Plata in the middle of beautiful Buenos Aires, if you want to live in the midst of rural Normandy in the north of France, all these things are possible **if you**

plan well. If you plan poorly, if you put your desires ahead of any reasonable financial plan, you will **suffer** tremendously.

I have made the effort to give you information that I feel is helpful, honest and at times blunt. This is not a politically correct book. Instead it is a frank discussion on the pros and cons of moving abroad for retirement. I feel any other type of discussion is a **waste of time**.

Can you live well and affordably abroad?

Yes, you can live well, and if you do things **intelligently** you can actually maintain or improve your standard of living. But you have to be realistic. If you have not managed your finances well, and are dependent on your government pension, you will not be able to move where you want to. The more expensive foreign locales, such as Europe, Australia and New Zealand, are all out. The only realistic, sensible options are in Latin America and to a lesser extent Southeast Asia.

If you are determined to live a totally Western advanced economy lifestyle abroad, complete with a full range of hi-tech appliances in your beachfront home, and enjoying five-star restaurants on a daily basis, you had better be rich come retirement time. Retiring abroad successfully means immersing yourself in the **lifestyle** of the country you move to. It does not mean **exporting** the lifestyle you were used to back home.

So in short, yes, moving abroad and living well is possible. In our current economic climate, many people have seen their retirement savings destroyed or considerably depleted. Moving abroad is seen as a solution to maintaining one's lifestyle and **dignity**. This guide will help you achieve a rewarding life overseas through realistic and unbiased advice. Good luck and pleasant journeys.

CHAPTER ONE – REAL ESTATE

In general, buying a property abroad in a foreign country is a **bad idea**. How bad? Very bad. If you read investment literature you'll find that one of the words most commonly used to describe investments abroad of any kind is **volatile.**

Volatility, in this sense, means that an asset's price rapidly rises and falls. Property abroad, particularly in emerging economies, and even more particularly in the areas of emerging economies where holidaying real estate is sold, is extremely volatile. It starts out as comparatively cheaply priced in relation to its equivalent in developed countries, i.e. beachfront property is far cheaper in Baja California than Hermosa Beach, California. But then it rises rapidly in value.

The first buyers in who sell property soon after they purchase it are the lucky ones. Their success stories spread, and others get in on the game.

Real Estate

The assumption is always the same: that someone else will come along and pay more than you originally paid. And it's hard to argue with success. Buyer after buyer reports easy sales to another person. This is known as the **Greater Fool Theory**. In other words there will always be a greater fool than you, ready to buy your property and make you a profit.

I look at this as if it were a game of **musical chairs**. When the music stops, and there are no more buyers, you are stuck with a property that is rapidly declining in value. Soon you own a property that is worth far less than what you originally paid for it, and it will take years, if not decades, for the price to recover, if it ever does.

The story of Dubai

Perhaps one of the greatest examples in recent history of Westerners "investing" in property overseas in order to make a profit and losing their shirts is example of Dubai. I saw it first hand in my time there. I was fortunate to not be earning enough money to afford a property, which was probably the first red flag to any outside investor. If a local executive earning a decent wage is unable to afford even a basic apartment, the market is probably overvalued.

The second red flag came in the form of **lights.** Dubai sold apartments within **zones** to foreigners. These zones were the only areas where foreigners were permitted to buy property, and even then the properties could only be leased for a 99-year period. Not allowing foreigners to buy property except by lease is a common event in the developing world. It's a draconian way of preventing wealthy foreign companies from buying up cheap land en masse, but it has the nasty **side effect** of preventing small retired or vacation investors from having the same property rights as citizens.

Within these zones giant apartment complexes had been built, but only a few of the rooms ever had their lights on. Why? Most of the apartments had not been purchased by small investors. Instead they had been purchased by **speculators.** Speculators have no interest in buying property to live in it. Instead they view property as something to be sold to others in large chunks. When you see giant apartment developments being built within "zones" or in pleasant areas such as beaches or near golf courses or ski slopes, and no lights or other normal activity in them, run away...and fast! You are about to witness a real estate implosion, and it won't be pretty.

Investors in Baja lose their shirts

The **aftermath**, particularly in poorer countries, is unfinished buildings left to decay in the elements.

The worldwide recession that began in the United States in 2008 made many holiday spots, not just Dubai, suffer immense real estate meltdowns. **Baja California**, a popular vacation spot for Americans, saw a marked decline in real estate values in the wake of the recession. Unlike Dubai, where retirees are few, Baja has long been an area where American and Canadian retirees spend their remaining years due to its close proximity to home and beautiful beaches and great food.

According to an April 15, 2010, article in the Los Angeles Times, enormous developments such as the Palacio Del Mar are filled with would-be retirees and small investors unable to sell their properties **even at a substantial loss.** One investor who purchased a property at the height of the boom in 2007 for US$477,000 was unable at the time of the article three years later to sell his property for US$439,000. The losses were not limited to smaller investors either. The famous **Donald Trump** created a development known as Trump Ocean Resort Baja with individual units going for as much as US$3 million. All remain unsold.

No recourse

To make matters worse, if you feel you have been duped into buying a property overseas after being fed exaggerations or even lies by a property developer you will usually have little to no recourse.

Recourse comes in the form of a court settlement, and courts in the developing world are spectacularly slow and corrupt. If you combine that with the **enmity** shown foreign plaintiffs who bought land that is utterly unaffordable to the average person, you can expect little to no sympathy that you lost your shirt to a local.

Not really an owner

A British friend of mine "purchased" land in Indonesia with several friends in order to build a small resort. The resort had two A-frame huts built on it and was located on an island in one of Indonesia's many archipelagos. In pictures he showed me, it was gorgeous.

The problem was that though he was the caretaker, he was not the owner. Instead of buying the property in some kind of government-condoned lease, he and his friends made a deal with a local to purchase the property in the local's name. When shown the money, the local Indonesian readily agreed.

Of course he agreed, because as soon as he got the money, he disappeared. This was not known to my friend, who went on and built huts and other elements on the island, **an island he did not even own**. His only recourse was the local Indonesian courts. As of this writing, five years after our initial conversation, he is still without a solution. **Never buy property abroad, particularly for investment purposes.**

Financing is usually not available

Perhaps the biggest problem facing someone who wishes to buy or long-term-lease a property abroad is the **lack** of financing. Many countries' banking systems are so corrupt and inept that they are unable to offer mortgages on properties. This means that to purchase a property you have to pay for everything up front.

Even if you can get financing, it is typical that the terms greatly favor the local bank. The terms typically are 30-40% up front, with the balance due in a very short period of time (like a year), or upon completion of construction if you are buying into a development that has yet to be completed. And if you come from a country like the United States that allows you to deduct the interest on your mortgage from your income tax, you will soon learn that no such deduction exists for the purchase of foreign property. No one is going to **supplement** your purchase abroad, particularly your home nation.

The fact that you, as a foreigner, are unable to get a bank to do a credit check and give you a reasonable mortgage (or a mortgage at all) says a lot about that county's economic stability. Do you really want to park substantial equity or money in a country you can't trust? The peace of mind that comes from the fact that you can leave at any time with little loss is worth far more than any piece of property, in my opinion.

Foreigners out!

As I mentioned before, you are not really an owner when you buy land in many countries. In the Persian Gulf, Mexico, the Philippines, Thailand, Indonesia, and a host of other countries, you are not allowed to own land unless you are a citizen. Typically these laws were passed to prevent **neo-colonialism**, or the return of rich Westerners who instead of using force to take over countries would instead use currency. While not allowing foreigners to purchase land has to some extent limited foreign investment in poorer countries, it has also limited exploitation, at least in the minds of citizens of the developing world.

Leasing as a solution?

The political leadership of many of these countries have come to realize that restricting foreign ownership means hindering foreign investment, and they have sought in various ways to overcome this problem by allowing long-term **leases**.

But as anyone knows who has leased a home, a car, or even an appliance, you don't really own the asset; you are simply renting it for a long period of time. At the end of the lease, control of the property reverts back to the original owner, which is usually the government that first issued the lease.

Typically these leases are offered in small zones, as I mentioned above. The problem with having property built in special zones that are separate from the rest of the land in the country is that these zones induce real estate **bubbles**. Bubbles mean rapidly growing prices quickly followed by enormous declines in value. Most people who buy into a bubble lose everything once it **pops**, or suffers a sharp decline in value.

The other issue with leasing is that as the years left on the lease decline, so does the value of the property. Who would want to buy a property that will revert back to the original owner in only a few years? A good example of this phenomenon is the area of **Marina del Rey** in Los Angeles. While this is not a foreign city, is has the same legal issue as any leasehold. Marina del Rey is beachfront property right next to Los Angeles, owned by the County of Los Angeles. The apartments there are quite cheap, yet ideally located. Why are they so cheap? Because when the development was first created, it was placed on a giant leasehold that reverts back to

Los Angeles County ownership when it ends. Why pay top dollar for a property that won't be yours in less than a decade or two? And why pay top dollar for a property that no one will be willing to buy from you at all in the future?

Complex legal structures in place of buying property

Another method used to buy property in the developing world is the creation of a complex legal structure that gives a foreigner some of the rights of a citizen in terms of property ownership. In Mexico, for instance, foreigners cannot purchase land on the beach or on the border. However, by creating a Mexican corporation, and having two shareholders, a foreigner can then have the corporation purchase property on the foreigner's behalf.

However, even these trusts have time limitations built into them that require renewal. If the government or the people decide that they've had **enough of foreigners** buying their prime land and bidding the prices up, you can bet that a law will be passed forbidding the renewal of the trusts. Another difficulty that might arise would stem from trying to sell this trust-bound land. If I was a foreigner deciding to buy land, would I buy land that only had a few years left on a trust? Or would I buy land that required me to create a fresh trust with a new set of time limitations? Probably the latter, and the latter won't be sold by you, it will be sold by a local citizen. The very purchase of a property by a foreigner may drive the value down slightly.

Signs of trouble

Unfortunately, most information on the internet or in books regarding moving overseas is linked to real estate agents in those countries who are **utterly lacking in scruples or ethics**. They will assure you that the real estate market in their country is safe and secure.

Real Estate

I suggest the following list of red flags that will show you that buying a property in the country you are planning on moving to is dangerous:

- No right for foreigners to **actually** own land
- Court system seen as corrupt and incompetent
- Aggressive sales tactics by local real estate agents
- Large, unfinished apartment blocks with no signs of habitation being built all at once
- Prices rapidly rising and unaffordable for most locals
- No financing available for purchasers
- Real estate agents largely unlicensed

This is your retirement and **nest egg**. Can you really trust it to someone you barely know? A far wiser alternative to buying property overseas is renting.

Property is an anchor

One of the biggest problems with owning property is that **it makes you stay in one place.** By that I mean that you cannot just pick and up and go if you want to move back home or move to another country. You need to sell your property first. Property has the funny characteristic that when you **really** need to sell it, you're either not able to sell, or you have to sell for less than what you paid.

What makes a person sell property? Usually money troubles. A loss of a job, a loss of income, and you will have to sell. But if your problems are related to an economic downturn, you can bet that everyone around you will be suffering as well. And that means that everyone around you will be selling their property at the same time. When the property market is overloaded with properties for sale, buyers are few and far between.

It would actually be better for you to sell a property for your own personal reasons, rather than economic ones. But even then, if the issue is health-related and you have to return home for treatment, you will not be around to sell your property. You'll be at home hoping someone is successfully selling it for you.

And what about popular unrest? If a country is unstable, and you have to leave to avoid getting swept up, you can't take your property with you. Even if the unrest isn't too great, it will certainly scare off potential foreign buyers, and the locals won't have the money to purchase your real estate. When you rent, if you leave unannounced or in a hurry, the only person who loses is your landlord. And there probably isn't a thing he can do to you if you leave the country never to return.

The renting solution

With renting you may feel the property you are living in is not truly yours. But if you think of the lease agreements you would be signing with the government in order to "buy", you would not really be an owner in any form. Remember, at the end of the day in the eyes of a foreign government you are not a citizen but a **guest**. Guests can have their **invitations** revoked at any moment.

Renting from a local landlord gives you one enormous advantage over a foreign property owner/investor: the **ability to leave** at a moment's notice. In my opinion the ability to get out of a foreign country with no delay is the most crucial ability to have when you live and retire abroad. At any given time the country you are living in may

- Pass laws that restrict foreigners' right to live in the country
- Erupt in revolution

Real Estate

- Suffer an enormous weather disaster that destroys thousands of homes near you and kills tens of thousands more people
- Devalue its currency, wiping out the value of the property

Think it can't happen? As I write this book in 2010, the most popular retirement destination for Americans, Mexico, now is home to the city with the highest murder rate in the world, Ciudad Juarez. Its entire northern border with the United States is largely in the hands of drug lords. Thailand, another popular retirement locale for Westerners, particularly Europeans, is paralyzed by anti-government protests that have resulted in considerable **violence and instability,** with the future of its government in doubt.

Scenes of expats fleeing into their local embassies have been shown on television countless times during our lives. While I am trying not to overstate the dangers of living abroad in order to deter you, I am simply stating that it would be in your best interest to make as little investment in the local economy as possible. You need to be able to flee if you can, and plowing hundreds of thousands of dollars into a property will **cloud your judgment** and make you unable to make to make important decisions when the time comes. Renting takes care of that. The repercussions from breaking an agreement with a local landlord are far less than the repercussions of losing your life's savings.

There is also the benefit of being a **foreigner** and renting. In many countries with a history of socialist governments, there are typically a great many tenant protections. Eviction in these countries is usually exceptionally difficult for a landlord, and tenants take full advantage of these laws. A foreigner, on the other hand, is seen as a temporary and wealthy potential tenant. As a foreigner you may be able to get better deals, and certainly will be responded to by a larger market than a local.

You may also have to pay **slightly more** rent than a local if you're not careful, but considering the fact that you have moved abroad to be in a cheaper country, you may still be able to save significant sums of money.

Renting is not without risks. Most people who offer a house to rent may see renting it out as only a temporary situation. They may intend to sell at some point in the future. (An apartment owner will more likely view his property as an income producing asset and will prefer to have long-term tenants. The selling of the property will be far less likely.)

Moving frequently is a huge inconvenience and renting a property leaves open the possibility of being forced to move. But in my opinion there is a substantial difference between **moving** house and **fleeing**. The former you do when your lease ends, the latter you do when you have to abandon a property you own.

If you will only feel comfortable in a house rather than an apartment, I suggest researching who the larger rental property owners are in the area where you wish to move. If they own several homes or villas, they will probably view these properties in the same way they view apartments, and you will less likely be forced to move due to the sale of the house.

What kind of property should I rent?

I think there are three important rules when it comes to determining what type of property you want to rent.

1. Rent an apartment, not a house. Apartments are cheaper, easier to clean, put you closer to your neighbors if you need help, and are more centrally located. A landlord is less likely to sell it from underneath you as well.

2. Pick a unit on the ground floor. As you get older, steps will become a hassle and a safety issue. Ground floor units allow for quick escapes in the event of a fire. Elevator repair is not the best in many parts of the developing world.

3. Choose an apartment near the places where you shop and more importantly near a quality hospital. Being close to attractions should be less of a concern. You'll probably get bored of them after awhile anyway. Being close to a hospital can save your life.

4. Make an inventory of everything included in the property. If you ever leave and want your security deposit back, you'll have the inventory to prove to the owner that you haven't taken anything. The inventory should also describe the **state** of everything included in the apartment in order to show that any damage on an item of furniture was there before you took it.

5. Make sure any apartment or house you choose has the **views** you want. You might get tired at staring at an alleyway or construction site. Make sure you find out if anything is going to be built nearby in the near future. Construction projects have a habit of taking a long time, particularly in the developing world. They can also obscure what was formerly a great view.

6. Are the utilities in working order? Do you get hot water from every tap? Is the stove gas or electric? Is the heater adequate? **Air conditioning** may not be available, or may be only available in expensive rentals (Americans may be shocked at this).

7. Find out what **amenities** come with your rental. Do you get access to a gym, a pool, or garden? Are these requirements for any place you might move into?

8. Ask neighbors about their experiences in the neighborhood, or if you choose an apartment, their experiences in the building. Are repairs done on time? What is the general state of the building and area?

Where should I rent?

It all depends on what you can afford, and perhaps more importantly, what you are **comfortable** with. If you decide to live among expats, you will pay more, often significantly more. When I lived in Bahrain, I chose to live not in an expat neighborhood, but with locals in order to save money. I lived in a villa on a dirt road. While I paid less and had much more room than most expats, I was away from the city center and away from native English speakers. I was also nearer to scenes of occasional popular unrest by rioters. It could be uncomfortable, though Bahrain is largely a safe country.

If you live with locals in a developing country, you experience some of the same **challenges** they will experience. The same could be said for living in a rural part of a developed country. It might be a shock you are unused to. Weigh the pros and cons of expenses versus being comfortable with your surroundings.

You may not have an option **at all**. If you do not speak the local language you won't be able to find more affordable listings in newspapers or other periodicals that are written in the **local language**. Real estate listings in English that cater to expats will always be more expensive than the listings that cater to locals.

The lease agreement might not protect you

A lease agreement has varying degrees of legal protection depending on what country you choose to live in. I'm not an expert in the legal systems of every country, but in my experience living overseas, the more developed the country, the more rights the tenant has. In a lease agreement you should make sure that there is a clause in the agreement that prevents the owner from **selling the property without giving you adequate notice**. Again, some jurisdictions may require an owner to give you first rights to buy the property, some may not allow the owner to throw you out before the lease period ends, and some countries may not enforce tenant rights at all. The poorer and more corrupt the country you move to, the greater the likelihood that the owner of the property you rent will seek to sell it if property values rise considerably. At that point you become a liability.

If a country has a corrupt or incompetent legal system, getting recourse to prevent being thrown out, or to prevent being forced to pay for damages you didn't do is unlikely. The lease agreement will carry little weight. As a retiree expat you will find that time is on the landowner's side, not yours.

However, when entering into a lease agreement, you should go over the terms carefully to determine if there is anything unfair or unrealistic. If you rent a furnished apartment, make sure that all furniture items are listed in the agreement. Make sure you determine how often you can have guests over and whether you can sublease at all. Are pets allowed? Which bills are you responsible for and which bills is the owner responsible for? What date is the rent due?

What if I don't see the property as an investment but want to buy anyway?

I still think it's a bad idea. The only advantage I can see to buying a property over renting a property in the developing world is that you don't have to deal with the possibility of a landlord arbitrarily throwing you out of the property and ending the lease. While that is a factor, there are many problems with owning a property in a poorer country:

- If the property is destroyed by a storm, a riot, fire, or some other catastrophe your insurance company may refuse to repair or rebuild it

- The local government may take back the property through some version of eminent domain
- You may need to leave the country and return home for some unexpected reason and don't know when you can return
- The property may have some type of construction flaw that is prohibitively expensive to repair

If you think these things can't happen, think again. Governments love arbitrarily taking property, particularly in developing countries. An article in the British paper, the *Guardian*, from March 28, 2010, describes the situation in Goa, a beautiful former Portuguese colony that is now a state in India. Goa is well known for its beautiful beaches and for its laid-back and carefree lifestyle which has attracted thousands of Westerners seeking to live like flower children in an Eden-like paradise. The global economic downturn in 2008 dramatically lowered housing prices, and locals called upon their government to remove Westerners they felt were offensive to local culture. The Indian government complied by restricting foreigners' ability to sell their properties. Confiscation of some properties has also occurred, and many properties had "their residential permit revoked" according to the article. Goa is increasingly seen now as corrupt and dangerous by many in the expat community. For those who invested substantial sums of money to own homes to for retirement, the dream is over.

Can insurance protect me?

In terms of insurance, Americans have had a tough time getting insurance to pay out after a disaster, namely the Katrina hurricane of 2005. Do you think that after a hurricane has blasted through your Caribbean neighborhood insurance companies will pick up the tab for you? **Probably not.**

Real Estate

While I cannot analyze in this book the quality of housing in every developing county that retirees move to, I think it is safe to say as a general rule that the quality is not on par with the first world. That doesn't mean you can't live in a wonderful home, it just means that in the case of a fire or earthquake, your home is unlikely to be able to withstand as much damage as a comparable home in the developed world. One of the leading causes of death in earthquakes in emerging economies is **poor home construction**. In 2010, a magnitude 7.0 earthquake in Haiti killed over 230,000 people. An earthquake of nearly the same magnitude in 1989 in the San Francisco Bay area killed 63 people. While it is unlikely you will retire to a country as poor as Haiti, you will probably retire to a country poorer than your own, and the number killed by any disaster will be considerable.

People who recommend buying property

When doing research on buying property abroad, I strongly suggest ignoring anyone who recommends it as an investment, or recommends it all. I believe I've laid out a very strong argument as to why you **shouldn't** buy property abroad. What do you have to gain that renting won't give you as well? There are many benefits to living abroad, but many drawbacks too. Minimize the latter by not buying property, and be aware of anyone who says it's a "great deal", and "safe". History moves quickly in emerging economies, and so does the value of property.

If you must buy

If you simply must buy, I would avoid newer properties and go for an old one. Why? Older properties that have been standing for years have routinely survived whatever cataclysm occurs in the country. If there is an occasional hurricane, tornado, or earthquake, the old building was built in such a way that it withstood it. The newer building is untested, has been built quickly to make a profit, and is built to local building standards rather than developed-world codes. In the event of giant disasters, it is the new buildings that quickly collapse, while the older ones that were originally built for the wealthy stay standing.

Beware the unlicensed real estate agent

When dealing with a real estate agent in a foreign country, demand to see the agent's license. If the agent does not have one or reassures you that his license is back in the office or somewhere else, **run – don't walk – away.** Unlicensed real estate agents are a surefire way to buy a property **without a clear title**. This is probably the biggest problem expats face in the purchase of property. While even a licensed real estate agent can give you a property that lacks a clear title, you can bet an unscrupulous con artist with no right to be selling property couldn't care less if he sells you property that is rightfully held by an orphanage. The other thing to be worried about: many unlicensed real estate agents aren't locals, **but fellow Westerners**. Find someone who is happy with his home purchase and ask for a recommendation as to which estate agent to use. Don't find one on your own.

Of course if you are going to buy property in a country where real estate agents are not licensed at all, I wish you good luck. You'll need it!

Lack of clear title

As I mentioned previously, lack of clear title is the **biggest issue** facing homeowners abroad. Title disputes are common in every country, but in countries that have only recently allowed expats to buy land, or are opening up a new section of the country to foreign investment, title issues are commonplace. Remember, the legal system, particularly in the developing world, tends to offer no recourse or solution for you unless you are willing to bribe your way to victory. And even then the wheels of "justice" will move exquisitely slowly. My original advice to not buy property still stands!

Building and repairs will take forever

If you are crazy enough to not only buy property, but to build a home as well, you can expect an immense number of **permit** issues, which in a sense are really bribes to the local municipal government. In the developing world you can expect them to be for arbitrary and fickle requirements, because the local government will view you as a potential source of revenue. By building a home you have essentially labeled yourself as a Westerner with a bit of cash, and you have become more of a target. For that reason I would suggest the easier route of purchasing an older existing property, rather than a new one.

If you've ever worked with a contractor or building supervisor in the West, you can imagine that in the developing world, or abroad anywhere you don't speak the local language, the challenges will be immense. Any repairs that will be done, and you can rest assured that repairs will need to be done, will be **time- consuming**, and possibly costly. The expats that I know who have had to wait for a villa or apartment to be constructed have all told me that if they had to do it over again, they **wouldn't** build new.

What about buying property in the developed world in places like Spain, Portugal etc.?

While many of the warnings I have given you concerning buying property in the developing world are less relevant in the developed world, even in places like **Spain, Portugal and Florida** you see much of the same volatility in housing prices. In any area that is reliant on new home construction and tourism, the local economy is one of feast or famine, depending on the state of the world economy.

The Financial Guide to Retiring Abroad

The problem with buying a retirement property in places you think are safer and more developed is that you will be **more inclined** to view your property as an investment. But the rapid fluctuations in housing prices will ruin any investment possibilities and have other nasty side effects. An article in the British paper, the *Guardian*, from July 24, 2009, entitled "End of the Dream for British Expats in Spain," describes the aftermath of a severe housing crash in Spain for British expats:

"For some, Spain has become a nightmare. Judy and Bill are going back to the West Country this month. Both served in the armed forces, then ran a fish-and-chip shop before coming to a rented villa with a swimming pool and views of the beautiful Jalón Valley in northern Alicante. That was two years ago. Frustration, boredom and their own naked prejudice are driving them home. Encounters with Spanish housing developers and their British estate agents – who scare them so much they do not want their real names used – have left them bitter. 'This is a country with no law,' proclaims Judy. 'We in England abide by the rules but here they don't bother. Even the Brits here rip you off. I think most people would go back if they could. It'll be a relief to get home. It's not as cheap as people think.'"

The fact that you might have chosen a country with a **stronger economy** than say a Latin American or Southeast Asian one can be a double-edged sword. In the wake of the Great Recession, the pound weakened against the Euro, making Spain more much more expensive for British expats, particularly those who were living on pensions that paid in pounds. The *Guardian* article goes on to describe an enormous number of vacant houses in the small seaside towns that were largely populated by British retirees. As vacant developments become eyesores, real estate prices will sink further.

Real Estate

Again, all these examples serve merely to warn the reader of the potential for disaster if you buy property. Regardless of how safe or wealthy you feel the country you live in is, a random course of bad events can change everything. Save yourself from potential strife and rent instead.

I will say this to those of you who insist on buying property abroad: see if the local banks offer mortgages. The best sign that a country has a stable financial system, and a strong legal system for disputes is whether its banks offer fair and competitive mortgages for property buyers, particularly foreigners. So if your new country offers a reasonable mortgage of say **15 years or more, at a reasonable interest rate, with a fair down payment**, then it might be OK to buy property. If your new country's banking system offers no mortgages or a mortgage of a very short duration, **buyer beware.**

CHAPTER TWO – PRACTICAL MATTERS

While the bulk of this book concerns financial planning in regards to retiring abroad, I think I'd be doing the reader a disservice if I didn't discuss some of the little things that can affect moving and living overseas. I consider this chapter a **potpourri** of valuable ideas that don't really fit into the remaining chapters of the book. The discussion in this chapter comes from my own experience living and working overseas, as well as discussions with other expatriates I have met in my travels. If you think such advice and information are too trivial for your attention, feel free to skip this chapter.

Language

It is possible to not know the language of the country you're moving to and do fine. I don't speak Arabic and have lived in two separate Arab countries. Granted, almost everyone in those countries spoke English, and in Bahrain there were thousands of my fellow Americans living on a giant

Practical Matters

naval base, but speaking the local language would have helped immensely. How? It would have **saved me money**.

The best reason I can think of for learning the local language is the day-to-day savings you will experience interacting with local merchants and businesses. For instance, taking a cab might become remarkably cheaper. If you speak the local language well enough, you'll be able to bargain for a better fare (particularly in the developing world), and you'll be seen not as a tourist but as either a local or someone who understands the intricacies of local life. Tourists get ripped off, natives don't. If you don't know the local language and are dependent on English-speaking businesses, you can expect to pay considerably more for everything.

The other big reason to learn the local language is **legal**. For every contract you sign, for every court case you're involved in, you're going to wish you spoke the local language. Contracts that are professionally drawn up always contain labyrinthine language designed to confuse and protect the contract drafter. In a court case proceedings will always be conducted in the local language, and never yours. Knowing the local language can be the difference between jail and freedom.

That's not to say you absolutely need to learn the language. You can get by with a **pidgin** version of the local language making use of some local words and hand gestures. It's very easy to do this, and I've certainly done it in my travels. But more importantly you should pick up the locals' hand gestures and actions yourself. This will enable you to sense danger, and to sense if you are getting ripped off or betrayed. I view language as a sort of **awareness** of what others are doing around you. The better you understand the language, the more aware you are of others' behavior and actions.

The best way to learn a foreign language is to **immerse** yourself. That means talking to people other than your fellow English- speaking expats. It means making friends with locals, dealing with merchants on a face-to-face level, and taking language lessons. Most countries have language immersion courses that cater to English-speaking foreigners. These typically last a week to a month and cost only a few hundred dollars per session.

Driving

One of the biggest issues in living abroad is the change in driving styles. This is particularly true when comparing the developed world with the developing world. Typically on developing world roads you will find:

- Many drivers who regularly speed at deadly rates
- Drivers who rarely or never use turn signals
- Drivers who rarely follow street signs, or obey stoplights
- Drivers who throw trash out their windows, most commonly cigarettes
- People crossing highways as they would an intersection (and regularly getting killed for it)
- Accidents, including lethal ones, a very common occurrence

Driving in the developing world takes lightning-fast reflexes, and a thorough awareness of all that is going on around you. You must be an experienced defensive driver, and you must drive aggressively or you will be run off the road. In many countries it is typical for a person speeding to tailgate your car and flash his brights, signaling you to get out of his way. There is very little concept of road manners or safety.

This is a **serious concern** to someone who is used to driving on relatively safe highways back home, and more importantly, **who is seeing their**

reflexes and eyesight deteriorate due to age. Though it is a concern, it is rarely if ever discussed in retirement guides. While a complete overview of automotive safety is beyond the remit of this book, it is important to know some basic guidelines:

1. The **bigger** the vehicle you drive, the safer you will be. The counter to this is that in a crash the larger vehicle is more likely to kill the other participant. I am going to avoid a debate on the ethics of driving a large vehicle like an SUV or pickup, but simple physics tells us that a larger mass smashing into a smaller one is likely to do the smaller vehicle considerable damage. A bigger vehicle **driven responsibly** will cause other drivers to steer well clear of you. Another added benefit of a large vehicle with considerable ground clearance is that it will be able to traverse open ground more easily, which is a consideration for living in a poorer country.

2. Make sure the vehicle you buy has **electronic stability control (ESC)**. According the National Highway Traffic and Safety Administration, ESC reduces accidents by 35 per cent. ESC is a computer device that detects when your vehicle is about to skid, and applies the brakes in order to steer your vehicle away from a skid. Skidding a vehicle usually means a loss of control and a possible rollover of your vehicle.

3. Watch out for animals on the road, particularly those that are being herded across by a shepherd. This is obviously far more of an issue in rural areas, but there are dozens of animals that regularly cross roads in order to graze or find water, such as sheep, camels, goats, horses, llamas etc. Smashing into them in your car will do far more damage to your vehicle than you can imagine. In addition to that, if you have killed an animal owned by someone else, you can bet that

you will be liable for the animal's death and that you will face a heavy fine and a possible court appearance.

4. Obey traffic laws **but only as long as everyone else does.** It doesn't make sense to follow the speed limit in a third world country when everyone around you is speeding. Going slow when others are going fast will turn your vehicle into an **obstacle** and you will be hit from behind. This is probably contrary to almost everything you've been taught, but then again driving in a third world country is illogical and borderline insane anyway. There is a sense of fatalism in all drivers in these countries that have long since abandoned even the pretense of safe driving. When in Rome...

5. It makes more sense to obey the **laws of the jungle** when it comes to driving in a developing country. These laws include the periodic bribery of traffic cops, speeding to keep up with the traffic, driving aggressively, and ignoring street signs if obeying them would mean endangering your life.

Other guidelines that are obvious but bear repeating are that you should always wear your seatbelt, that you should always keep your eyes on the road, and that you should avoid doing anything to distract yourself. That could mean talking to a passenger, using your phone etc. While I have instructed you to copy other drivers around you, you should only copy those behaviors that will save you. You must be **a better driver** than those around you. If the people around you in traffic are chatting on their cell phones while speeding, you should speed but not chat on the phone as well. You need to be more aware than the next guy, and instead make mental notes on his stupid behavior so you prevent him crashing into you.

My solution to the dilemma of driving abroad is that you consider **hiring a permanent driver**. By hiring a driver I mean hiring someone with their own vehicle, rather than hiring someone to drive yours. That means if your driver gets into an accident while driving you, since he is the owner of the car, he will be liable instead of you.

Every country has different cultural **idiosyncrasies** when it comes to driving, and only a native will know them all. I feel that this is such an important issue that you should put into your **budget** before you move abroad. The most dangerous daily activity almost everyone does is to drive a car. In poorer countries, that danger is magnified dramatically. Scary statistic time: According to the WHO, traffic accidents are the leading cause of death for 10-24 year olds, and 600 people a day are killed in traffic accidents in China. I can tell you from my own experience in the Middle East that the combination of cheap oil and high-performance cars made surviving the drive to work every day unharmed a miracle.

Hiring a driver has the added benefit of possibly helping you **avoid traffic.** Poor countries and countries experiencing strong economic growth (as is more typical in developing countries than developed ones) tend to have horrible traffic congestion, as road-building and public transport cannot keep up with the growing numbers of cars being put on the road. A driver will know all the various side roads and alleyways you can drive through to avoid traffic and get to your destination on time.

I am not a big believer in having the **license** of the country you are driving in. I believe an international license combined with your passport is often **good enough.** There may be considerable disagreement with me on this issue, but I feel there is a certain power and prestige to flashing your passport, particularly if it is from a wealthy country. I had to appear before a traffic cop at police station after an accident that was largely my fault while I lived and worked in Bahrain, as was the law for any accidents that occur. I did not have a local driver's license, but I had a license from a neighboring Gulf country which was valid, and I had my own license from the United States. I also had my passport. The traffic warden found in my favor though it was very debatable as to who was at fault. I believe, though I have no way to prove this, the fact that Bahrain is the home to a large U.S. naval base and thousands of American sailors got me off. The other person's insurance had to pay for the accident. Other readers may have experiences that have led them to a different conclusion, however. Your passport, and a bribe, may be enough to get out of any accident that police are involved in.

It is for this reason that you should keep your home driver's license for as **long as possible**. I will discuss later in this book the importance of keeping a home address for billing and healthcare purposes. Keep it as well to be able to maintain your driver's license. Your license is a valid form of identity, and saves you the need for lugging your passport (a far more important document) around with you. I feel it is a get-out-of-trouble card in many countries, and it shows a police officer that you are probably a competent driver (even if you are not).

The rules are entirely different in the developed world, and of course traffic laws should be followed there. Bribing traffic police and ignoring signs should be avoided at all costs. While I understand that this part of the book is almost completely devoid of politically correct discussion, and you could argue that I am advocating breaking the law in poor countries, driving is such a dangerous and yet necessary part of life that I feel it would be irresponsible of me to write anything less than what I see as the truth, particularly when it comes to the safety of others.

If you feel you must absolutely buy a car, then **buy a car brand that is popular in the country you where you choose to live**. If you retire to Mexico, you will find that while Nissan and Volkswagen are popular,

Practical Matters

Toyota is not. In the Gulf, where I resided for three years, the most popular brands were Toyota, Peugeot, and Chevrolet. Buying a brand you that is uncommon or imported into the country you live in will mean **costly repairs** and **a bad or small dealer network** that will be hard to get to when you need to do repairs. The key is to find out which companies actually **build the cars in the country**.

For instance, if you choose to live in a Latin American country that has a Chevrolet factory that builds a certain car, buy that **exact car.** The car will be cheaper since there are no tariffs on it, and replacement parts will probably be cheaper as they will most likely be built locally too. The car will be popular because of its low cost, making repairs cheaper and better, as mechanics will have more experience repairing the car.

When I was living in Dubai, to save money I bought an Opel Astra in Sharjah, the neighboring Emirate. The problem with the car was that it was an **unpopular** vehicle for the region. It was small, and a hatchback. In a country where the price of gasoline is little more than a dollar a gallon, people want big cars and big SUVs to drive. I was forced to sell the car at a loss (relative to what I owed on the vehicle) when I had to move countries for work and ended up selling the car to an Azerbaijani used car trader who specialized in taking unwanted vehicles to his native country and re-selling them on the grey market there. He made a hefty profit on my low mileage car, I did not. If my car had been more popular, I would not have had to deal with this issue.

I also suggest that you **do not import a car** on your own. The costs associated with this are usually high. Not only do you have to pay shipping expenses including insurance, you also have to pay import tariffs. In many developed countries, importing cars yourself is next to impossible due to safety restrictions. Developing countries may see an imported car as a vehicle that competes with vehicles built by their own factories and will tax it heavily. **Buy locally**.

Finally, if you must buy a car for whatever reason, make sure to buy one that is **cheap,** because of the effects of bad roads on your vehicle (less of an issue in the developed world). The nicer the car, the more horrified you will be when you see the scrapes caused by road pebbles tearing tiny chunks out of your new paint. Always remember that a car is yet another asset that can be broken into or stolen, and the nicer the car is, the juicier the target it makes for potential thieves.

In regards to **auto insurance**, I believe you should always have it, even if owning it is not enforced in the country you live in. It is in the poorest countries that the traffic accident rates are highest, and if you live in a poor country, you will at some point be involved in an auto accident. Insurance brings peace of mind, but more importantly, it will lower repair costs for a car that has been damaged in the all-too-regular occurrence of traffic accidents. In some countries, like Mexico, if you are involved in a traffic accident without insurance, regardless of who is at fault, you can be held by the police without trial until fault is determined.

Television

For many who retire abroad, TV is the last thing on their minds. For others, like myself, being away from your favorite sports team is painful. It simply isn't the same reading scores on the internet. Local cable television and satellite are frequently **not adequate.** Their content is dependent on the company that runs them, and they are unlikely to give you the channels you want to see. If you are fan of American sports, or regionally-popular sports like cricket and rugby, you will not find your teams televised in a country that primarily plays soccer. The best solution I can think of is streaming videos on the internet. Of course the quality of these will not only depend on your computer, but **on the bandwidth access** of the country you live in. Various commercial websites have thousands of films and movies available for free but with commercials, and of course it might be possible to access your favorite sport's website for streaming video. Typically you will have to pay for those.

If there are considerable numbers of your nationality, you might try the local pub or bar that caters to expats to see if they will air your favorite sport. For television and film, Hollywood fare is easily available through **illegally copied DVDs** in much of the developing world. Most EU countries will not allow you to travel back with these, and they will be confiscated. The United States is far more liberal and allows you to have one copy of each movie you have purchased but no more. I won't say any more on the matter as all these tactics for acquiring media are quite unsavory.

Hygiene and sanitation

If you are new to living and traveling abroad, you might be unaware that many countries, particularly poorer ones, have issues with personal hygiene and sanitation. While there is little you can do about others' personal hygiene, except grin and bear it (and bear it you must, for you will be surprised as to how much other people can smell), there is something you can do in regards to sanitation.

One of the biggest issues with sanitation in the developing world is the continued dumping of **untreated sewage** into bodies of water that people play in. In countries that are experiencing substantial **economic growth**, infrastructure is overstretched, too many people are moving in, and sewage systems overflow. In the mind of local government, the best solution is to build a pipe from developments to the nearest body of water.

This is particularly true with **new developments**. Since developers are usually closely associated with the corrupt government, their goal is to build units first, and worry about infrastructure later. These new developments are the biggest culprits in polluting bodies of water with sewage.

The only solution I can think of is to move near a body of water that is surrounded by older developments that have been built to cater to locals, rather than expats. Either that or avoid the water as much as possible.

These aren't the best choices, but in many countries where pollution is endemic, you have to make do the best you can.

Earning a living overseas

Most retirement books will lie to you and tell you there are ample jobs overseas in retirement locations. If you consider manual labor to be an adequate job, then the books are correct. Starting a business is another idea commonly bandied about. Starting a business in the developing world is extremely difficult, and will require **bribes**, **ruthlessness**, and the expectation that your customers will steal from you at every opportunity. In my experience overseas, the only times Westerners successfully started businesses were when their clients were **other Westerners.** The dynamic of doing business in the developing world is quite different from doing business in the developed. For instance, if a supplier or customer does not pay a bill, you usually have essentially **no recourse.** The court system will either never get around to hearing your case, or will automatically favor the local citizen over you.

If you could create a business that either exported something from the country you lived in to your old home, or created a website that dealt mostly with customers from your home country then you might have a feasible business plan. But any other efforts are probably doomed to failure. And if you think about it, there's a logical reason for it. Poor countries' economies **don't work very well.** Customers steal, suppliers don't deliver on time, bills go unpaid. If it's hard for the locals themselves to start a successful business, why should you succeed? If you cannot afford to move abroad without having some sort of successful local business, I would suggest **not moving abroad.** Falling into debt in a developing country is typically a far more serious offense than falling into debt back home.

The other issue with starting a business overseas is finding suitable **employees**. If you start a business abroad, I highly recommend that it be the type of business you run either by yourself or with the help of your immediate family only. Employees are not only a hassle in and of themselves, in most countries the paperwork required to hire and fire them is **overwhelming**. Expats from the United States will be shocked to find that in some countries it is almost impossible to let an employee go at all.

Remember that starting a business is inherently **risky**. Businesses fail a lot. Don't become dependent on your business for income, and don't put your pension into your business to help it survive. Look to create a business that will take up only a small amount of your time, and will act as a hobby rather than a new career. You are trying to retire, and in retirement work should come second to fun and relaxation.

In regards to getting a job overseas, you will face considerable **red tape**, as you are a foreigner. In most countries, finding work as a foreigner is difficult. It requires a **work permit,** and typically these work permits are only issued if the job is something that not many local citizens can do. This means jobs that require **highly technical** skills or jobs that **teach another language like English** are the only jobs available to expats.

While the former type of work is usually well paid, English teaching is not. If you lack the necessary skills to get a good job and can only teach a foreign language, don't expect to earn a decent wage.

If you decide to work before you are eligible for your state pension, you run the risk of **shrinking your contributions**. This will result in a **smaller benefit** when you are eligible for it during retirement. If you work abroad, make sure that it is only to supplement your state pension (Social Security for Americans), particularly if you are dependent on it for the bulk of your retirement income.

You may wish to forgo any red tape and simply work **under the table**, without the legal right to do so. Many expats do this, but it is risky. Remember, in many countries it is grounds for **deportation**. It is one thing to overstay your visa, it is another thing to take a job away from a citizen. You probably are safer with a low-paying job such as teaching English or tutoring, but for anything more substantial I recommend getting a work permit. Even if you are caught and confident you can bribe your way out of trouble (obviously this is only possible in a developing country), you should save yourself the pain and trouble and see if you can qualify for a work permit instead.

This is a common theme throughout this book: **avoid legal entanglements whenever possible**. A work permit is additional hassle, and makes you more dependent on local government authorities. That means potential for graft and/or bureaucratic nightmares. You should move abroad with the intention to be fiscally independent and not dependent on the local economy to fund your retirement.

Practical Matters

The importance of the internet

Besides acting as a potential television replacement, the internet can **allow you to make cheap phone calls**. Companies like Skype allow you to use your internet connection to transmit voice data just as you would a phone. In some countries however, companies like Skype are banned, and the monopoly phone system is the only way to make a call. To avoid this, I suggest using a **virtual private network (VPN).** A Google search for VPNs will show you hundreds of companies that will set one up for you for a small monthly fee. I used vpnaccounts.com a few years ago in order to access Skype when I lived in Dubai, where it was banned to force residents to use their expensive, monopolistic, state-run phone system. A VPN convinces your internet service that you are really accessing it from another country, and it allows you to bypass any server's restrictions. Any and all banned websites are now free to watch.

Another important aspect of the internet is it gives you the ability to **pay your bills and do banking.** If you move abroad you will have to rely on the local postal service, and it will probably be inferior to your home one. This will be particularly true if you choose to live in a rural area. I would suggest handling as much of your postal and banking needs online as possible.

If you decide to live in a rural area, particularly in the developing world, you will probably need to purchase **satellite internet**. While almost all countries have Wi-Fi access in every city center, in rural areas high speed internet access is a rarity. The problem with satellite internet is that it can be **very expensive**. I believe it is worth it, particularly if you do your banking online and make international phone calls via VoIP.

Depending on where you live in the world, you must use a particular service, as only certain satellite internet providers have satellites over given continents and areas. Satellite internet services are usually a few hundred dollars (U.S.) per month depending on how fast a connection you wish to purchase. VoIP works well even with low speed connections, so you may be able to skimp on this expense to some extent if your sole purposes for internet access are bill-paying and phone calls. However, satellite internet requires a somewhat steep initial fee in order to be sent the necessary equipment (an actual satellite **dish**) which you will probably only lease for the duration of your contract with the company.

If you decide to live in **North or South America** the following companies offer services: Skycasters, Enterprise Satellite Solutions (ESS), and VSAT Systems. This includes the Caribbean. VSAT Systems does not cover southern Mexico. IsoTropic Systems covers almost the entire world.

Bentley Walker covers only South America. Elite Satellite only covers North America and the Caribbean.

For **Europe,** the following companies offer services: Avonline, IsoTropic (though not in all of Eastern Europe), BusinessCom (only Eastern Europe and not all of Western Europe), GlobalTT, and Bentley Walker. For **Asia,** BusinessCom offers comprehensive coverage. For **Oceania**, DigitalSkys covers Australia, but not all of New Zealand.

This list of providers may not be complete but should give you a good start. In areas with more providers you should expect more competitive pricing, and in areas with fewer providers, you should expect higher costs.

Mail

Before you move, find out if the country you are moving to has a decent postal system. If it does, don't bother with using a mail forwarding system but just have everything sent to your new address. If it doesn't, you will have to either find a mail forwarding system that is reliable, or depend on someone you trust to send you your mail. You may find that relying on a close relative to take care of your mail is an incentive to communicate with that person regularly. Obviously if you have anything you are unwilling to let anyone know about coming to you in the mail, you should not do this. You could also try the company **Earth Class Mail** which will read your mail and convert it to email. They are easily found through a Google search. I have friends who have used the service, but while it is good, it is also expensive.

There is however, another incentive to keeping a home address. The United States has very strict rules for its citizens when it comes having a **foreign bank account**. Many banks, if they determine that you are living overseas and not in the United States, will cancel your account for fear of inadvertently assisting someone in hiding money in an offshore account or helping a **terrorist**. It is **not illegal** for Americans to live abroad, but it is more difficult than for citizens of other developed countries. In order for you to maintain your bank account, I suggest you maintain an address back home. I do not mean a P.O. Box. Depend on someone you trust to collect at least your bank statements. It is not the best situation, but until laws are changed to make it more amenable for Americans to live abroad, it is a situation you will have to live with.

Banking

No matter where you live, you will always need the services of a local bank branch. As with many aspects of retiring overseas, there is a set of rules for developed countries, and a set of rules for developing countries. When moving to a developing country, before going abroad I would find out which **banks from your home country** have established themselves in your retirement destination. If you do not have an account there, I would open one. By having a home country bank account and a retirement country bank account at the same bank, you can more easily transfer funds back and forth, avoid ATM fees, and more importantly, there is less of a possibility that **your bank will collapse.** A local bank is far more likely to collapse, and to take your money with it. Local accounts are hardly ever insured in the case of bankruptcy or insolvency. With a large bank that is based in your home country there is the possibility, **not guarantee,** that your money will be insured by your home government even though it is abroad.

One example from history I came up with was as follows: When the communists came to power in Russia in 1917, they seized the local branch of Citibank, then called First National City Bank. The depositors who managed to get out of Russia sued Citi in the U.S., but the courts backed Citi, and Citi never made good on these deposits.

An alternative that I have not investigated, but have read about and think shows promise, is to open an account in your home country at a **bank or other financial institution that does not charge ATM fees**. With a card issued by this financial institution you could travel anywhere in the world, and use any ATM without hassle. However, make sure that this deal is one that is permanent. In many cases the offer is only made to attract customers, not to be a permanent part of the bank's marketing strategy. If the rules are changed when you are abroad, you'll be in trouble.

Another important factor in choosing a bank is whether you can conduct **online banking**. Make sure that the bank you choose has a reliable online setup that you are comfortable with and that will not lose your money if you make transfers and the like. Many poorer countries' banks are not online, which can lead to difficulties. Virtually every bank in the developed world is on-line, except the very smallest. Choose only those that are online for your banking needs. You will avoid a paper trail in the event of a move, and you will be able to organize yourself far more efficiently.

For this reason, you should keep **as little of your money as you can** in a developing nation. In the event of a financial collapse, hyperinflation, or some sort of government action that freezes your account, you want to lose as little as possible of your nest egg. The safest thing you can do is to leave the bulk of your hard-earned money at home where it will more than likely be safe.

In Mexico in the 1970s, banks offered accounts where the deposits could be had in dollars. This was seen as a way of attracting Mexicans to make use of the banking system which was (and is) notorious for routinely collapsing. The idea was that dollar denominated deposits were actually worth something, and that deposits denominated in pesos threatened to dissipate in value in the event of hyperinflation.

However, the Mexican government saw through this stunt and dollar deposits were **force-converted** into pesos when the peso was devalued to combat hyperinflation. This action has happened recently in other countries such as Pakistan and elsewhere in recent years. The lesson is this: If it's in a foreign bank, denomination in your home currency will not be enough to save you.

When moving from one developed country to another, the safety of banks is far greater, and you probably shouldn't worry about losing your money in the event of a bank collapse. While European countries may not guarantee their depositors' accounts, the events of the recession of 2008 show that all Western European countries will do whatever it takes to prevent a **bank run** or loss of depositor confidence. It is one of the many signs that a country is developed that it can insure the protection of money invested in its local banks. The reason for that confidence is to attract future investment from abroad and from its citizens. Developing countries, sadly, are not in a position to offer such **reassurances** and you should use caution in leaving your money to their care.

In many countries it is exceptionally difficult to even open an account. Letters of reference may be required, as well as credit and background checks. In many countries it may take a considerable period of time. This is probably the most important reason that you keep your old bank account open indefinitely. Closing your account and hoping to open a new one overseas will mean holding onto considerable sums of cash for a long period, which is always a **risky** prospect.

Offshore banking

There is another type of bank account that is relatively easier to open than a standard checking or savings account overseas. Offshore bank accounts are seen by many as an ideal way of hiding money from their home governments in order to avoid paying tax. While tempting, I believe opening these accounts is very dangerous.

Western governments, particularly those of Germany, the United Kingdom and the United States, have all made increasing efforts in recent years to crack down on their citizens who are hiding money in offshore accounts. **It is often illegal to have money stashed in offshore accounts and not report it to your government.** In the United States in particular, it is illegal. The days of the successful businessman being able to elude the tax man are coming to an end in this new era of increased government oversight of the financial sector in the wake of the recent market crash. Avoid becoming a casualty and report all income from foreign sources if you are required to do so.

Practical Matters

Credit cards, debit cards and cash

In the developed world we are seeing a move away from a cash-based society to one that is solely focused on credit and debit cards. The developing world is just the opposite. **Cash is king**, and while there is a slow movement towards cards, I would advise you to rarely if ever use them. If you must use them, use your credit card rather than a debit card. Why? Every time you use a card of any kind, you risk an unnecessary charge being added to your bill, or even worse, your card being **cloned** and used by a thief. The latter has happened to me while living abroad. If you use a credit card, you can dispute the charges and not pay them. Credit card companies also tend to be more agreeable when it comes to reducing or removing charges. With debit cards, on the other hand, there are far fewer protections, and lost money **is taken directly out of your bank account**. Trying to convince a bank to put back money into your account is quite a challenge, particularly if it's a foreign bank.

Another issue with the use of cards is the fact that you have to rely on a working bank network. When you use a card to pay for a meal, the restaurant swipes the card in a scanner that dials your bank by phone to confirm whether it can charge for the meal. If your bank's network is down for the day due to technical difficulties, your card won't go through. **This is a common occurrence** in the developing world, even in upscale parts of the world like Dubai. You do not want to get stuck being unable to pay. Once again, cash is king.

Live like a local, not a Westerner

If you try to live like a Westerner in your retirement country, unless you are wealthy, you will quickly run out of money. In my opinion, living like a Westerner means buying **imported goods.** Unlike in the West, particularly the United States, countries cannot run up huge trade deficits and receive cheap goods from exporting countries like China. Instead they have to make do with what they have, and in order to protect their own industries, will typically slap tariffs on imported goods. The consequence of this is that things like **televisions, cars, computers, portable electronics and books** are very expensive relative to their cost in your home country. Whenever possible, I suggest going without them.

That means no television in **every room.** Only one car for your family, rather than one for every member. If possible, go without a car and use public transportation or be driven to destinations by a local. You might also skimp on the purchase of a dishwasher and dryer, and instead do it yourself or hire someone else to do it. Appliances are very expensive to purchase in most countries. If you **must** have a particular item, such as a computer, purchase it before you leave.

Buy locally

In general, you should avoid buying anything **imported** when living abroad. Only in countries like the United States, and perhaps parts of Northern Europe, can you buy cheap imported goods. Most developing countries slap high tariffs on cheaply-produced goods from countries like China in order to protect their own industries. In plainer English, that means that locally-made goods will always be substantially cheaper than foreign products.

Buy locally means **eat locally** as much as possible too. Westerners would be shocked to realize that many of the tropical fruits and vegetables they eat back home are imported. To import an exotic fruit or vegetable to your new home in the developing world will be tremendously expensive. Learn to eat what the locals eat, and enjoy it. The more of your old life you import, the greater your expenses will be.

Practical Matters

Learn to use products not sold in chain stores, such as so-called hypermarkets like Carre-four, Asda, Walmart, etc. but goods produced just down the street. For instance furniture built by a local artisan would be perfect for your home. When negotiating to rent a property (or if you're foolish, buying a property), the owner will always include furniture as part of the price. **Immediately say you do not want furniture**, and use that as a bargaining chip. You can easily replace beds, tables, chairs and rugs with goods produced locally for very little. It's exactly the same place the owner bought his furniture as well.

Alcohol is probably one of your biggest expenses if you decide to import it. If you insist on having your favorite beer or liquor every evening and it is imported, you can be sure to run into budget trouble. Try the local stuff and save money. Unlike drinking water from the tap, alcohol kills germs, and will probably be safe to drink regularly. Will it taste better than what you're used to? Who knows? If your consumption is reduced, all the better, for the sake of health. What is surprising about importing alcohol is how easy it is for people to forget how a mere drink can be so expensive. Unlike an appliance or furniture or a car, alcohol in terms of price per liter is extraordinarily expensive. In fact, far more expensive than almost anything you can think of that could be imported. Buy accordingly.

Air conditioning

Perhaps the most expensive thing you can splurge on is **air conditioning**. The current drawn from an air conditioning unit, particularly a centralized air conditioning system, is immense. For Americans, who are used to the constant flow of air conditioning, living without it is quite a challenge. For other Westerners, air conditioning is also an expensive luxury.

A common alternative are **wall units** that are placed in every room that requires cooling. These have the advantage of being cheaper because instead of cooling the entire house, they cool only the room you are in. They have certain drawbacks, though. In my experience using them in the Persian Gulf, they tended to create moisture and drip water down the wall, peeling paint and if on the second floor of a house, dripping it into the room below. They also periodically break, and are not as **reliable** as central air.

The final alternative is of course a **fan**. An electric fan constantly blowing is not nearly as pleasant as air conditioning, but you can be confident that you, and virtually everyone else in your new country are using one too.

Air conditioning is a great expense. And with electricity somewhat intermittent, with **frequent blackouts** and brownouts during summer months because of poorly-built and overloaded local electrical systems, you will probably have to rely on a hand fan periodically anyway. My advice is to acclimatize yourself to living without air conditioning, particularly if the county you are moving to is known for an unreliable electricity supply.

Bribery and corruption

In the developing world, bribery is a part of life. In fact, in countries where it is rife, it is a significant part of the economy. Many times police forces make much of their salaries from local bribes that come in the form of "fines". These are arbitrary and on the surface will seem unfair. I would **avoid arguing** about them. The key I have found to bribing a policeman is to settle whatever issues there are right at the scene of the problem. Instead of demanding to go to the police station or to appear in front of a magistrate, **pay the bribe now**. By dealing with more police officers and public officials, you risk having to pay more "fines" and bribing many more people. The fewer people you bribe, the cheaper you can get off.

Practical Matters

There is an interesting index known as the **Corruption Perception Index (CPI)**. The index is published each year by Transparency International, a German NGO that seeks to raise awareness about international corruption and the issues related to it. The index looks at "the degree to which corruption is perceived to exist among public officials and politicians" according to its website. Here are the top ten **least corrupt** countries, with the least corrupt at the top:

1. New Zealand
2. Denmark
3. Singapore
3. Sweden
5. Switzerland
6. Finland
6. Netherlands
8. Australia
8. Canada
8. Iceland

The reason for the duplicate numbers is that some countries scored equally on the scale. I've listed below the rankings of several of the more popular retirement destinations for Western expatriates:

24. France
25. Chile
25. Uruguay
27. Cyprus
32. Israel
32. Spain
35. Portugal
63. Italy

66. Croatia
75. Brazil
84. Panama
89. Mexico
106. Argentina

What is interesting is that in the top ten is a country that is by no means totally democratic (Singapore), and there are developed countries such as Italy scoring far lower than developing countries such as Uruguay and Chile. Dictatorships I have lived in, including Bahrain (46) and the UAE (30), score well, though I believe the index is overweighting **street-level corruption** which is low in those two countries, and underweighting **institutional corruption** which is high there. I define street level corruption as the corruption a person faces on a daily basis. That would include the bribery of police, staff at a company, or any low-level civil servant to get what you need.

Institutional corruption I would define as corruption that allows the wealthy to do as they see fit, either due to the fact that they are related to or closely associated with government leaders, or because they are in fact the leaders of the government!

Street-level corruption is the corruption that **will affect you the most**. Because it involves dealing with police officers, taxi drivers, office staff, etc., it will put a strain on your daily budget. High levels of street level corruption are both a drain on the local economy and a **hidden tax**. They also require you to become skilled at **haggling**. You will need to bargain with police, taxi drivers will not use meters and demand a deal for whatever route you want to take, shops will never give you a set price that is fair. For someone from a developed country, it can be **very exhausting**. If you are unused to such behavior you might wish to reconsider moving o these types of countries. Countries that that score in the 40s or higher on the CPI I would consider to have high levels of street level corruption, as well as institutional corruption.

Institutional corruption is what it sounds like. It is corruption of the major institutions that make up a country. This is far more prevalent than street-level corruption, and is far more **insidious**. It means that a person living in a country with high levels of institutional corruption will only be able to rise so far unless he or she is **related** to someone in power, or **knows** someone in power. It means there is little recourse if you wish to take on an institution you feel has wronged you. **The most common way expats get on the wrong side of institutional corruption is when they buy property.** When you buy a property in a corrupt country, you have little or no recourse if the property is defective, quickly loses its value, or has fees associated with it that rise dramatically.

The second most common way expats get on the wrong side of institutional corruption is when **they are employed in a corrupt country**. This will occur if they feel they have had their work visa arbitrarily revoked, that their employer has treated them unfairly, or that they have not been paid on time or at all. Usually they find that they have little or no recourse, particularly if their employer is a powerful organization within the country.

If you wish to avoid institutional corruption, the best thing you can do is to **limit your interaction with the government of that country.** That means involving yourself contractually only when absolutely necessary. Avoid signing property deeds, avoid contractual relationships with locals, and avoid having to tangle with any bureaucracy. Make use of your own embassy instead whenever possible. Of course filling out the forms necessary to rent a property, get a visa, and receive medical care are all things I highly recommend that you **do not avoid**.

Moral laws

Depending on where you come from in the world, you may have to adjust your behavior somewhat to your new country. What might be acceptable on a Friday night out after a few drinks could be seen as very **sinful behavior** in another country.

In my experience abroad, the most pressing example that comes to mind was during my time in Dubai. A British couple was caught by Dubai police allegedly having sex on a beach late at night. After several months of house arrest, followed by considerable media scrutiny in the Gulf and in Britain, the pair were given a suspended sentence and deported. The woman, who worked in Dubai, was fired from her job. In most developed countries little would have occurred if the police had come upon the couple.

The biggest problems expatriates get into abroad are usually drug and alcohol-related. While alcohol use is tolerated in many countries, drug use is almost universally seen as a very **illegal act**. In countries like the United States, and some parts of Europe, marijuana has largely been decriminalized, or legalized for medicinal purposes. However, in most other parts of the world, it is an act punishable by a severe sentence. Even in countries where it is widely done, it is a risky act.

The consequence of drug use being seen in such a negative light by the international community is that if you are caught using drugs, your home government may not assist you as strongly it would in the case of other crimes. There are thousands of Western expatriates languishing in third world prisons for drug offenses. The recent case of a British citizen expat executed at the end of 2009 in China demonstrates the willingness of the developing world to punish all drug users equally and brutally.

Overt displays of affection, vulgar gestures, spitting etc., these are all behaviors that must be minimized when traveling abroad. "Rights" are not universal. What you believe you have the "right" to do in public may not be allowed in every country.

Drugs and crime

Throughout the developing world, particularly in Latin America, drugs and the drug trade have taken an **immense** toll. Crime related to drugs, particularly in countries like Colombia and Mexico has skyrocketed. Currently, Ciudad Juarez, a large city in the north of Mexico, has the **highest murder rate** in the world, higher even than war zones such as Baghdad and Kabul.

A retiree must realize that if he or she moves to Latin America, particularly Central America and Mexico, they are moving to countries that are at times extremely dangerous. In the case of Mexico, the most popular retirement destination for Americans in the world, the drug war has destabilized the country, and made many northern cities **no-go zones**. In these areas, the Mexican government has all but ceded control to local drug lords.

The drug trade is a booming business that is growing by leaps and bounds due to the insatiable appetite for cocaine, marijuana and methamphetamine by Americans and to a lesser extent Canadians. Central America has become the largest conduit of drugs in the world into the United States. With cheaply grown drugs selling for hundreds of times what it cost to make them, the profits are **enormous** and have fueled drug empires stretching across the North and South American continents.

All of this has made a stay in much of Latin America more **problematic**. My suggestion is to stay away from cities that have been ceded to the drug cartels. Avoid using drugs yourself. And most importantly, learn what you can from expats in the know who can give you a better picture of what is really going on in the country.

In a country such as Mexico, the power vacuum created by drug lords displacing government control in certain regions has allowed a new type of criminal to emerge. **Kidnappers** are a potential threat to expats who make their home in Mexico, though they have by and large only targeted Mexicans and/or Americans of Mexican descent. Kidnapping has skyrocketed throughout Mexico, and people of means are being targeted.

The purpose of these kidnappings is quite simple: **ransom.** For many criminals, the drug trade is either too competitive or not profitable enough, and in true entrepreneurial spirit, they have discovered a new and at times very profitable revenue stream. For expats, this means you should **watch out!**

As of this writing in 2010, there has yet to be an incident of a foreign American or other national being kidnapped for ransom. I fully expect that to change in the near future. It is for this reason that I encourage expat retirees to select a country to live in other **than Mexico**. While I will continue to write about Mexico in this book for completeness's sake due to the large number of Americans and Canadians who retire there, I cannot in good conscience recommend it as a retirement destination.

While the drug trade has increased crime throughout Latin America, it has not increased it to the extent in Mexico. Other Latin American countries are still **relatively** safe destinations, for now.

Racism/Provincialism/Prejudice

Any discussion of moral laws must also coincide with a discussion about racism and prejudice. It is often the case that a poorer country will have provincial attitudes towards behaviors that are tolerated to a much greater extent in the developed world. When learning about your new country, determine through interviews with other expatriates whether they have experienced racism or any form of prejudice. The closer to your own ethnicity the expat you interview is, the better.

In many countries, what would be considered racism by some, would be seen as humorous by others. Throughout Latin America, and even in Spain, **caricatures** of blacks are found in cartoons and on the packaging of various foods and candies. The caricatures would be seen as deeply offensive in the United States and elsewhere. It is also common in Latin America to refer to someone by a prominent physical feature in a friendly way. This would be unacceptable in much of the developed world.

In my own experience as someone of mixed race heritage (I am half Mexican/half Scottish), I have found that the world is remarkably less racist than is commonly assumed. I myself have never experienced overt hatred for the way I look in my travels abroad. Of course my experience may be unique.

Much of what could be construed as racism is simply ignorance. There is also a difference between ignorance and overt hatred. Ignorance is common, while overt hatred against someone because of the way they look is uncommon. Virtually every ethnicity has examples of wealthy, successful individuals, and many of the old stereotypes that certain ethnic groups were poor, dumb and uncivilized have diminished as everyone in the world slowly emerges from poverty.

Homosexuality and retiree destinations

Gays and homosexuality in general are frowned upon in the more religious and poor parts of the world. Sadly, many popular retirement destinations in the developing world are **potentially unsafe or unfriendly** for gay men and women. While Mexico City has legalized gay marriage, much of the rest of Latin America has been slow to follow. Evo Morales, the President of Bolivia, recently discussed how the eating of hormone-fed chickens might be a leading cause of homosexuality, so you can imagine how well gays are viewed in that country.

I believe it is safe to assume that a country that allows gay marriage or civil unions is probably a safe destination for gay retirees. As of the year 2010, the following countries around the world allow gay marriage:

Sweden, South Africa, Norway, Canada, **Spain**, Belgium, South Africa and the Netherlands. Only Spain would I consider a popular retirement destination for expatriates, and I have bolded it, though some say South Africa is also being seen as a retirement destination particularly for British expats.

I consider countries that give the right of gay marriage to be more gay-friendly than countries that only allow **civil partnerships, common law marriages**, or other legal marriage contracts for gays. Legalizing gay marriage means that the local government has ignored the protests of religious leaders, and has given gay couples the same rights as straight couples, whereas a civil partnership is accepted only by the government and not by religious leaders.

The following countries as of the year 2010 allow some sort of civil partnership for gay couples: Hungary, Austria, **France**, Ecuador,

Practical Matters

Australia, **Uruguay**, **Switzerland**, Slovenia, Andorra, Luxembourg, **New Zealand**, **Portugal,** Germany, the United Kingdom and Denmark.

The following countries as of the year 2010 allow for common law gay marriages: Czech Republic and **Croatia**.

A civil partnership has **more** legal weight than a common law marriage. Traditionally, a common law marriage simply meant that a couple was considered married if they had cohabited for a period of time. You can see how that might result in legal problems if you have difficulty proving cohabitation for whatever reason. You could rightly view a country that has only legalized gay common law marriages as one with **inferior** gay rights protections, compared to one where gay civil unions or even gay marriages are legal.

Essentially, gay-friendly countries fall into a **five tier** system: countries that allow gay marriage, countries that allow civil unions, countries that allow common law marriages, and finally **countries that prohibit gay marriage, and countries that prohibit homosexuality** altogether.

The two bottom tiers are countries that gays should approach warily. Typically, countries outside of Western Europe either give gay people fewer rights, or openly discriminate against them. My advice to a gay person **is to avoid countries that openly discriminate against gays**. These countries are typically found in sub-Saharan Africa, and parts of Asia. They are also typically found in Muslim countries as well.

Of course gays are everywhere, even in countries where homosexuality is prohibited. As I am not gay, I am unable to give a clear picture of which countries tolerate homosexuality more than others. I will say that in countries where it is prohibited, you can expect to find no **clubs or bars** out in the open for gay clientele. In countries where homosexuality is tolerated but gay rights are not protected, you may be hard-pressed to find establishments that openly cater to gays. In all of these countries there is the potential for violence against gays, and the arbitrary closing down of establishments that secretly serve gay customers.

Sadly, many of the countries of Latin America and East Asia that cater to expat retirees fall into the category of countries that tolerate or discriminate against gays, mostly the former. Below is a list of select countries that are considered retirement destinations and what the current status is of their treatment of gays under the law:

Mexico: Homosexual acts are legal, but gay marriage only legal in Mexico City. Civil unions are legal in the state of Coahuila. There are, however, legal discrimination protections.

Costa Rica: Homosexual acts are legal and there are some discrimination protections in the law. Gay marriage and civil unions are illegal.

Panama: Homosexual acts are legal, but there are no protections under the law against discrimination for sexual orientation.

Argentina: Homosexual acts are legal. There are no national laws against discrimination based on sexual orientation. Civil unions in some parts of the country are legal.

Uruguay: Homosexual acts are legal. Anti-gay discrimination is banned. Civil unions are legal. (I would argue that Uruguay is the leading Latin American country in terms of gay rights).

Practical Matters

Malaysia: Homosexual acts are **illegal** and punishable by **whippings** and prison sentences of varying lengths. Gay marriage and civil unions are both illegal.

Thailand: Homosexual acts are legal. There are no laws protecting discrimination based on sexual orientation. Civil unions are not legal. (However, Thailand is renowned for its liberal attitudes towards homosexuality).

Philippines: Homosexual acts are legal. There are no laws protecting discrimination based on sexual orientation. Civil unions are not legal.

Spain: Homosexual acts are legal. Anti-gay discrimination is banned. Gay marriage is legal.

France: Homosexual acts are legal. Anti-gay discrimination is banned. Civil unions are legal but gay marriage is not.

Italy: Homosexual acts are legal. **Some** anti-gay discrimination is banned. Gay marriage, civil unions are all illegal.

Australia: Homosexual acts are legal. Anti-gay discrimination is banned. Civil unions are legal in only some territories.

New Zealand: Homosexual acts are legal. Anti-gay discrimination is banned. Civil unions are legal.

Dominican Republic: Homosexual acts are legal. There are no laws against discrimination on the basis of sexual orientation. Gay marriage and civil unions are both illegal.

Barbados: Homosexual acts are **illegal** and punishable by prison. There are no laws against discrimination on the basis of sexual orientation. Gay marriage, civil unions are both illegal.

Bahamas: Homosexual acts are legal. There are no laws against discrimination on the basis of sexual orientation. Gay marriage, civil unions are both illegal.

Nicaragua: Homosexual acts are legal. There are laws against discrimination on the basis of sexual orientation. Gay marriage, civil unions are both illegal.

Ecuador: Homosexual acts are legal. There are laws against discrimination on the basis of sexual orientation. Civil unions are legal.

Brazil: Homosexual acts are legal. Civil unions are legal in Rio Grande do Sul. There are laws against discrimination on the basis of sexual orientation.

The treatment of women

For the female expat retiree, moving abroad in many ways is more of a danger and a challenge than it is for a man. That is not to say that a woman can't find **immense enjoyment** from living abroad. I simply think that a woman should tread a little more carefully, particularly in the developing world. Women's rights are new to much of the globe, and the status of women in most societies is, unfortunately, not equal to that of men.

How do you measure how well a country treats women? You can look at various elements such as access to education for women, whether women have the right to vote, and how large pay gaps are between men and women. Are there many female political leaders in the country you are looking at? How long is female life expectancy versus male life expectancy? Are women dying in childbirth at alarming rates? All of these factors play a role in determining the status of women in a country.

While some of the poorest and most religious countries in the world tend to discriminate against women horrendously, many of the countries in this guide are either strong in the area of women's rights, or are progressing well. The United Nations has developed an index, the **Gender-related Development Index (GDI),** that takes the mathematical equations that are the foundation of the famous Human Development Index and adds many of the statistical factors affecting women that I wrote about in the previous paragraph.

I've listed the rankings for some of the more popular retirement destinations for expats according to the GDI for 2009 (the most recent index), along with the top ten countries on the list to give you an idea of how close (or far) the country of your choice is to giving women equal rights to men:

1. Sweden
2. Norway
3. Finland
4. Denmark
5. Netherlands
6. Belgium
7. Australia
8. Iceland
9. Germany
10. New Zealand
11. Spain

18. United States
19. Portugal
21. Italy
24. Argentina
27. Costa Rica
39. Mexico
47. Panama
59. Philippines
63. Uruguay
67. Nicaragua
68. Malaysia
76. Thailand

Scandinavian countries dominate the top and this continues the trend internationally that Scandinavian countries are the most equitable to their citizens in many different respects. Latin countries, even those in Europe, score far lower. I feel he list is a little too biased towards countries that have put women in political positions. Many countries with terrible records on women's rights, such as Pakistan, have had female leaders, but they could hardly be called equitable towards women. The treatment of women within a country's upper classes and political elite will often be very different within the middle and lower classes.

This list cannot measure the day-to-day treatment of women in a country. In some countries it is perfectly acceptable for men to make catcalls at women they find attractive on the street. In more conservative countries, particularly those that are Muslim, such catcalls are totally socially unacceptable, but you would hardly call those countries leaders in the area of women's rights.

Disabled access

If you have mobility issues due to a handicap, or are in any way disabled, you may find it difficult to live in many countries, particularly if they are poor. While developed countries have passed **laws** guaranteeing that many businesses must allow access to disabled customers, the age of many buildings makes implementing these laws difficult. Oftentimes a business will conform to the law, but just enough not to get into trouble. Such a result is hardly ideal.

To a disabled reader, or someone with a disabled spouse or family member, retiring abroad will be fraught with difficulties. Obviously, Europe and the United States will have the best facilities available as in both areas there are laws mandating **accessibility**. The more exotic locales will probably be out of bounds for many with disabilities.

If you wish to live in the developing world, some of the wealthier countries in Latin America such as Uruguay, Argentina, Mexico and Costa Rica will have more accessible restaurants and hotels, but finding an apartment or house to rent will be difficult. Check with realtors to find residences with previous owners/renters who had mobility issues similar to yours.

Sadly, there is little in the way of information on the internet for disabled expats overseas. The stereotypical expat is seen as someone who doesn't require anything in the way of special treatment and the dilemmas facing disabled expats are ignored. There is useful information for traveling abroad as a disabled person, but little in the way of information on permanent living abroad for disabled people.

My suggestion is to research and find out whether the country you wish to move to requires businesses to have handicapped access. Find out if services are available to help with mobility issues through the use of specially equipped vehicles to transport you. Poor countries often expect the extended family to take care of someone who is disabled, and this is not often an option for a disabled person from a Western country. In our part of the world government fills the gap.

Any move overseas for a disabled person will mean spending more money than the average expat will have to spend, in order to modify living quarters for accessibility. The cost savings found in the developing world can be rapidly eaten up through the employment of staff and to pay for changes to living space. My final suggestion is to avoid permanently moving to the poorest countries in the world, and to be prepared to not skimp on your budget in order overcome any challenges your new environment might present.

Street Crime

Crime is a very complex topic, and though it is a crucially important one, I can only touch upon it briefly here. In general, crime is low in the developed world, and high in the developing world (the United States is the notable exception). There is **overwhelming** evidence that the leading cause of crime is **poverty**.

Sadly, the countries that are poor are the ones where a retiree can spend the least amount of money and enjoy the best lifestyle generally. There are few, if any, countries where both a cheap lifestyle and a crime-free life are attainable.

If you move to the developing world, you can expect to at some point be a **victim** of crime. The greatest reason for crime is poverty, and the developing world is filled with impoverished souls. But what kind of crime do you have to fear? Most likely your residence will be targeted by thieves while you are away or you will be pickpocketed.

The same basic rules for keeping your home safe apply anywhere. Avoid leaving your cars or bicycles on the street. Lock all doors and windows. Buy an alarm system, as even the sound of it going off may scare away some thieves. But most importantly, don't let anyone know you have valuables, and if you have them, store them in as safe a place as possible.

Thieves target those who appear to have money, and if you live far better than the rest of the population and regularly wear jewelry in public, you can expect to be targeted.

Having a criminal background

If you have a criminal background, you may have trouble qualifying to retire to any foreign country. If the crime you committed was years ago, you **might** be able to be allowed to enter. If the crime is a minor one where you served only a brief time in jail, you **might** be let in. It all depends on the staff at the embassy/consulate/immigration board that is conducting the review and how they read the relevant laws that day.

In general, have a clean record. In today's hi-tech world, a background check can uncover virtually any dirt from your past. What you served time for and have all but forgotten about will seem like yesterday to an immigration officer. There are no repercussions for getting rejected because of a bad background, unless you are a fugitive, but if one country rejects you, expect all the rest to as well.

Alcoholism

One of the most pressing problems for expatriate communities around the world is the issue of alcoholism. Alcoholism is an insidious disease that strongly affects expats for several reasons. For one, some expat cultures have always promoted alcoholic consumption, and these expats have brought their problem with them. People from **colder climates** tend to drink far more than people from **warmer ones**. What may have been a worthwhile habit to combat cold and damp weather can quickly become a debilitating illness in a warm and alcohol-plentiful environment.

What expats who drink regularly need to understand is that they may at times be considered by locals to be drunks who can be taken advantage of, or to be a source of offense to the conservative locals. Many cultures look down on excessive drinking, or for that matter, drinking at all. Consider carefully whether your drinking could be a source of trouble for you in your new country.

Another popular cause of alcoholism is **boredom**. While you may have visited your retirement paradise in the past, you only stayed for a short period of time, no longer than two weeks. It never occurred to you that lying on a hammock day after day listening to the waves hit the beach could be so mind-numbing. To compensate, you drink. What was never an issue before in your life has become deadly.

Lack of activities is the leading cause of boredom. Many island nations or beach communities will in some sense **lack culture**. By this I mean that the local movie theater with subtitled or dubbed Hollywood action films will be your only cultural outlet. Many expats assume that immersion in a new culture is itself enough to keep your mind busy. It is not. When you move to that isolated beach or mountain, you are essentially moving to a place where most locals **do not want to live**. They've all moved to the city for jobs and culture. You have moved to what they **abandoned.** Keeping busy with hobbies, sports and trips is the best way to stay away from the bottle.

Practical Matters

Hiring help

If you decide to retire to the developing world, you will find that the cost of labor is cheap enough that you will be able to afford housekeepers, and possibly a driver and other assistants. The easiest way to find a housekeeper is to ask your fellow expatriates who they use. They should be able to recommend someone.

When hiring someone to clean up after you, I suggest hiring them to come only **once or twice a week**. Putting up someone in your home on a permanent basis requires substantial attention to that person's issues and problems. You'll need to supply him or her with furniture, food, bed linens, etc. A weekly or bi-weekly cleaning is enough for any lifestyle, and allows you to save on expenses. My experience with this type of hired help has been great. I would also include the washing of clothes in your helper's duties, but not ironing unless you are physically unable to iron yourself. Any clothes that require dry cleaning such as dress shirts, suits and other clothing should be kept in a place where the housekeeper cannot accidentally wash them and ruin them.

Sadly, when items are stolen the most likely culprit will be your hired help. Conceal valuables well. Even if your housekeeper has no intention of stealing from you, but mentions offhand to a friend the beautiful necklace she saw around your wife's neck before you went off to dinner, such an act can result in thievery. You must take extra precautions in an impoverished country. As a Westerner you will be seen as wealthy whether you are or not. Plan accordingly. Complain constantly about how poor you are, even if it isn't true.

As you get older and perhaps more infirm, the need for high-quality assistance becomes even greater. In the developing world, nurses can be hired cheaply, while in other developed countries in Western Europe and in places like New Zealand and Australia, the health services will provide high-quality health assistance, provided you can afford local insurance or are qualified for the public healthcare. My point here is that you must make sure that your nurses are from **reliable** and **trustworthy** sources. It is one thing for a housekeeper to steal from you; it is quite another for a nurse to take advantage of you when you are most vulnerable.

Moving your stuff

One of the biggest issues when moving abroad is the actual moving itself. The logistics involved in moving to another country are immense. I have a suggestion that may seem brutal to some readers, but I feel it is a necessary one: **move as little stuff as possible**.

In today's disposable society, we all have a tendency to **hoard** mementos and such. As a Westerner you are probably used to having a large wardrobe, a large set of dishes and tableware, and huge, comfortable beds. If you move the developing world, or if you are an American moving anywhere outside of the United States, you can expect to have to put up with smaller appliances, beds, rooms, houses etc.

In fact, if you move your stuff from home you may find it **incompatible** with your new country. **Voltage** is the most obvious example. Various countries use various voltages, and you will need adapters to run all your various gadgets. As we grow to depend on high tech "appliances" like Blackberries and laptops, changing voltage might result in the destruction of your device.

What is perhaps not as obvious is that moving things like **beds** can entail similar difficulties. Mattress sizes are not uniform throughout the world. Bed frames that are purchased locally may not fit your mattress, nor will locally-made sheets. Cars from abroad may use too much gas, or use the wring kind of fuel entirely. In Egypt natural gas is one of the more common fuels for cars. In Brazil ethanol is the most popular fuel. Your car may have to be converted at considerable expense.

The key to successfully living abroad is to live like a local as much as is both **reasonable** and **possible**. If you move to a developing country I don't mean that you must live in a shack with no running water. But I do mean that you should seek to copy the lifestyles of a local from the upper middle class and, only if you can afford it, the upper class. What constitutes upper middle class varies from country to country, but it means someone who takes full advantage of the low cost of living, and what is locally produced and manufactured.

Clothes

When it comes to dress when living in your new country, I suggest two rules. One, dress in such a way as to **not offend**. Two, dress as much **like the locals** as possible.

In terms of not offending, I would suggest that you dress according to the environment you are in. Beach wear should be worn solely at the beach in conservative countries. The vast majority of retirees who move abroad move to warmer climates. While going without a shirt and shoes (if male), or in only a swimsuit (if female) would be more permissible in a European or American setting, in other countries in the developing world it would be frowned upon. Your goal at all times should be to blend in, and not stand out, as you are a **guest** of sorts in your new country. Wearing what you feel is most comfortable can not only offend, it can also make you a target for crime, as it will reveal to others that you are a "well-off Westerner".

I also think you should dress like a local as much as is possible. Locals will buy locally-made clothes which **are cheaper**, in fact far cheaper, than imported clothes. Locally-made clothes will also be more comfortable and be made to withstand **local weather**. And again, looking like a local will make you look like less of a tourist/outsider and more like someone who fits in, which will help you avoid being targeted for crime.

There's one big problem with buying clothes locally, however. **They may not fit**. As a Westerner you are probably much bigger and taller than the locals. Shoes are probably one of the biggest issues, and shoes that fit big feet are hard to find outside the Western world. You may be forced to make a regular trip home to restock on clothes if you have too large a frame for local clothes. Fortunately, in the developing world **hand-tailored** clothes are remarkably cheap and can be made for your size. All my suits were hand-tailored in Bahrain, cost less than 100 U.S. dollars apiece, and have impeccable stitching. Materials, though, are not world-class but are decent.

Phone plans

When living abroad, the general rule concerning phone plans is to avoid using long distance as much as possible, and make use of local phones for local calls.

Voice over Internet Protocol (VoIP) companies, such as Skype, are the best solution to making long distance phone calls. If you use a VoIP company you will save a great deal of money. However, the problem with VoIP is that the **sound quality** is not good if you call with a regular landline from your computer. Using VoIP to call another person/computer using VoIP results in very good call quality, though. I have been in a situation where I was using VoIP to call a business in another country to save money, and I was apparently very difficult to understand to the other caller. Because the other caller was not tech-savvy, and did not make use of VoIP himself, I was forced to use a cell phone for an international call at considerable expense. If you make regular use of a VoIP system, be sure to buy the best possible **headset and microphone** in order to maximize the quality of your internet calls.

VoIP is a necessity in much of the developing world where corrupt governments have allowed a monopoly or near-monopoly to take control of the phone system and charge exorbitant rates. But for local calls, it is a nuisance as it is far more troublesome to make a phone call from your computer than from a phone. The newest cell phones coming onto the market have VoIP options, but they only work if you are in the vicinity of a Wi-Fi network.

Since you are largely dependent on the local cellular network to make local calls, I suggest **texting** as a cheap alternative to making an actual call. While texting might be seen as something teenagers do obsessively, it is a reasonable alternative to calls once you learn to type fast enough. Be careful not to say anything sensitive on your texts, as the phone company records them all!

Relationships
Moving abroad can strengthen or destroy a relationship. On a personal note, I have seen the expat community create many new relationships, and I have seen it destroy others. A new environment means new **stresses** for any couple.

Before moving abroad, make sure that your partner is on board with the decision. Both of you must be in complete agreement that moving away is the proper decision. Do either of you have elderly relatives who need to be cared for? Are both of you OK with not seeing your children or friends for long periods? Are both of you able to handle the changes in temperature or physical environment of your new home? And perhaps most importantly, are both of you used to seeing each other most of the day? Many couples who enter retirement spent most of their time apart as they went to work. Retirement itself means a completely new **dynamic** in a relationship, and combined with a complete change of scenery can lead to many problems.

If you are finding yourself spending far more time, or less time than usual with your partner, change your schedule to accommodate him or her. Communicate over any potential issues. And seek marital **counseling** if possible. Developing countries are less likely to have sufficient counselors available due to cultural prohibitions and simply inefficient healthcare systems, but with a little looking it is possible to find them. A successful relationship is one of the biggest keys to a successful overseas experience.

CHAPTER THREE – WHERE TO LIVE

It's time for some blunt truths: wherever you retire, unless you are very wealthy and can afford to live anywhere in the world, you will choose your retirement destination in part by how much you can take advantage of the **lower cost of living**. Even if you choose to live in France or Italy, or another developed country, it is very unlikely you will choose to live in hyper-expensive capital city. Rather, you will live in a rural village, once again, to take advantage of a lower cost of living.

There is nothing wrong with this. However, there is something wrong with the place you have settled, because if it was run well, it would **not be poor**. *The Economist* every year publishes its list of the world's most **livable cities**. In 2010 the ten most livable cities were the following:

1. Vancouver, Canada
2. Vienna, Austria

3. Melbourne, Australia
4. Toronto, Canada
5. Calgary, Canada
6. Helsinki, Finland
7. Sydney, Australia
8. Perth, Australia
9. Adelaide, Australia
10. Auckland, New Zealand

The Economist rates cities according to their political stability, level of crime, availability of goods and services and infrastructure. That being said, none of these cities are ideal retirement destinations for one simple reason: **they are expensive to live in.** While Australia and New Zealand could be seen as popular retirement destinations for expats, if you were to move there, you would almost certainly live in a rural area, far from those countries' cities.

A brief word about weather

Hurricanes are a yearly threat to many parts of the Caribbean and Central America. Unfortunately, many ideal retirement countries are located in an area known as the **hurricane belt**. The hurricane belt affects **every single Caribbean country** except Trinidad and Tobago, Barbados, Bonaire, Curacao, and Aruba. Within Central America, only Panama escapes harm. **All other countries in the region are in yearly danger of hurricanes.**

When do hurricanes come? They come mostly during the **Atlantic Hurricane Season,** which takes place from June 1 – November 30. September and November are when the most hurricanes take place. Whether you are a believer in global warming or not, it is undeniable that hurricanes have been increasing in their frequency and intensity in the last several years. This trend will more than likely continue. A tropical storm may have a slim chance of killing you if you live in the hurricane belt, but it may destroy your home and your assets. Think carefully before moving to the Caribbean to retire, or to much of Central America. The further inland you live, the less likely it is that you will suffer the effects of a hurricane.

Storms are an issue in any coastal environment, and particularly on islands. In the Philippines and other Pacific island nations there is a yearly **typhoon season** with cyclones forming from August to September, but due to the warm temperature of the ocean they can form at any time. In poor countries where **soil erosion** due to **deforestation** is commonplace, these storms can cause mudslides and flooding. Such events can displace and kill thousands.

I grew up in Southern California, and mudslides would periodically destroy and kill, but usually only those people **who built on the side of a hill**. While properties built on hillsides have spectacular views of the valley or basin below, they are also deadly and require considerable repairs after a mudslide or rainstorm. You can avoid the heartache that comes from watching your house fall into a ravine by living in a more urban environment and a flatter area.

Cost of living

Perhaps the most important part of your decision to move abroad will be the cost of living in your new country. It almost goes without saying that the cost of living in a developed country is usually far higher than in the developing world. However, oil-rich countries tend to be very expensive places to live as well. The Persian Gulf countries, Russia, and Kazakhstan have cities that are some of the priciest in the world. But these are not retirement destinations.

When moving abroad you must understand an **important trend** in the world's economy: **Everyone is getting richer.** Over the last couple of centuries the average person has become considerably wealthier. Over the past thirty years world GDP per capita has **quadrupled.** Virtually every country has seen its citizens become wealthier. Now that wealth, particularly in the developing nations, has not been distributed equitably, which is why there is still significant poverty in the world. But who could have imagined thirty years ago that the average person would have access (not necessarily ownership) to a motor vehicle, own a cell phone, and regularly watch television?

My point is that the country you move to in order to take advantage of a lower cost of living is more than likely getting wealthier year by year. As it gets wealthier, it will become a more expensive place to live. Tax rates will become higher as citizens demand more services from their government. The price of property will surge. Immigration will become a more pressing issue, with more regulation soon to follow. The inexpensive paradise you have found will become pricier.

And there's really nothing you can do about it. Besides, countries with negative rates of economic growth, like Zimbabwe, are usually very bad places to live. While they are inexpensive, they are also typically very poor and unstable. When you move into a country that you believe will save you money in the **immediate** future, make sure you realize that the cost of living will slowly creep up and chip away at your nest egg and lifestyle. The only real solution is have saved as much money as possible during your lifetime, and to **live within your means.**

Where to Live

Where you can live for less than US$1000 per month

Many retirees face the prospect of being forced to live solely on their government pension. They either did not save adequately during their career, or made poor investment choices and saw their money squandered. The only thing saving them from total poverty is that monthly government check.

It is for this reason that many Westerners move to the developing world for retirement. Europe is closed off to them, as are the developed countries like Australia and New Zealand. Latin America and Asia are the only possible locations. Below, by cost of living, I have listed the most affordable countries, from most economical to most expensive. Latin American countries such as Uruguay and Argentina have had currency devaluations in the last decade, so their currencies are valued poorly compared to the dollar and Euro.

1. Ecuador
2. Belize
3. Nicaragua
4. Argentina
5. Dominican Republic
6. Mexico (outside Mexico City)
7. Panama (outside Panama City)
8. Philippines (outside Manila)
9. Malaysia (outside Kuala Lumpur)
10. Thailand (outside Bangkok)

Asian countries, with their stronger fiscal discipline, mean more economic stability but higher cost of living. These are the tradeoffs. To live as cheaply as possible, you must live in a country that is relatively unstable and that occasionally defaults on its debt. As a country stabilizes over the years, expect it to get more and more expensive. As a country's wealth grows, so does the cost of living there. The correlation is direct.

You'll also notice in parentheses that the capital city is listed separately. That is because the cost of living there is typically far more expensive than the rest of the country. These cities are usually not the ideal place for a retiree. They are loud, pricey, and dangerous. Suburbs or rural areas around the capital are more ideal places to live. They are also too expensive to live on less than 1000 U.S. dollars a month. In the first five countries on this list it is still possible to live within city limits on less than 1000 U.S. dollars per month (but not recommended).

Learn your history

One of the biggest mistakes you can make before moving abroad and investing your hard-earned money into a new country's economy is to have little to no idea about that country's history, culture or government. In my experience, expats, particularly those who are still young and working, couldn't care less about what's going on with their new country's history or politics. I think that is both unfortunate and **dangerous**.

Not knowing that the country you wish to settle in has a history of government instability, or periodic changes to the laws affecting expatriates, can lead to serious problems. I suggest the following actions in order to learn about the country where you intend to settle and to help prepare yourself for possible instability:

- Read books covering the last 100 years of the country's history. Is there a pattern of coups, fraudulent elections, rioting, rebellion?
- Read the country's English language newspapers online. Read Google News daily with search parameters of the name of your

new country and the name of its leaders. International media might have a more unbiased opinion on your country's current issues.

- Make friends with locals. Talk to them about what's going on. You'd be surprised at how rarely the expat community does this. Find a local who is educated, speaks your language and can give you the insight necessary to see what's really going on in your new country.
- **Economic history** is just as important as political and social history. Argentina, a country growing in popularity with retirees, has periodic currency devaluations, credit defaults, and now high inflation. A search through the Financial Times or Wall Street Journal archives can be very helpful concerning economic news.

Understanding your new home is something that will take time. It's also something you should at the very least have a foundation in before making your final move. While a full-blown revolution is the worst case scenario, a far more likely occurrence will be economic instability. You can imagine the impact a currency devaluation would have if you were to **have purchased property**. Your investment could be wiped out.

The most important lessons you can draw from an historical understanding of a country are

- How great the odds are you will have to leave
- How much risk is involved in a substantial investment in the local economy
- The odds that your visa/residency/citizenship will be revoked

Does your country have racial classifications for citizenship (Malaysia)? Does your country have periodic currency devaluations (Mexico, Argentina)? Does your country have a history of political instability

(Thailand, Argentina, Panama)? These are the types of questions you should be asking yourself. Not just whether the beaches are nice, how the weather is, and what kind of food goes with which beer.

Look into the future

Understanding the country you are moving to will enable you to see **its future** more clearly. And I do not only mean its political future, but its **natural** future, for lack of a better term. By this I mean what will happen to the country in terms of weather and other naturally occurring catastrophes. **Polluted countries** are more likely to have soil erosion, which means **mudslides** after a rain storm. It can also mean air pollution which can aggravate a lung condition you might have. It can also mean more pollutants in the **air, water and soil** that can cause cancer or other illnesses. It's something you may wish to think about. Yale University and Columbia University have come up with an **Environmental Performance Index**. This index seeks to determine which countries are the most environmentally friendly through a number of factors including water, air pollution, environmental burden of disease, biodiversity and habitat, forestry, fisheries, agriculture and climate change.

In the Americas, the countries that scored the highest on the index were Costa Rica, Cuba, Colombia, Chile and Panama in that order. In Europe it was Iceland, Switzerland, Sweden, Norway and France. The Asia Pacific region saw New Zealand, Japan, Singapore, Nepal and Bhutan round out the top five. Countries with the highest scores tended to be in Western Europe, followed by Central America and then the Asia Pacific region. Countries in Sub-Saharan Africa and the Middle East scored very low.

The index is currently the only one of its kind, so its accuracy may be suspect. However, I feel it is a commendable effort to determine which countries are doing the most to safeguard their environment and consequently, their citizens and residents. I have lived in terrifically polluted parts of the world, including Bahrain (42 out of 100 points on the index) and Dubai (40.7 out of 100 points), with oil and raw sewage washing ashore on a regular basis, and I can assure you such an environment is not **conducive to good human health**.

Which are the nice countries?

The United Nations has made an effort to measure countries by **human development**, which is a nice way of saying which countries aren't dumps. The higher the country on their bi-annual ranking, the better it is to live in. The list makes use of a composite of several statistics such as **life expectancy, GDP,** and **standard of living**. Standard of living is measured by per capita income and poverty rate. While I believe the list has problems and ranks some countries too high (such as the UAE), I think that overall it gives the best picture of how well off a country is. This human development index (**HDI**) is shown in part below from its most recent compilation in 2007:

1. Norway
2. Australia
3. Iceland
4. Canada
5. Ireland
6. Netherlands
7. Sweden
8. France
9. Switzerland
10. Japan

Both Iceland and Ireland have probably fallen somewhat since this list was published because of the collapse of their economies in the midst of the global recession in 2008. But while this list is a little out of date it is still a good overview of which countries are pleasant places to live. Below are the rankings of a few of the more popular retirement destinations for Western expats.

15. Spain
18. Italy
20. New Zealand
34. Portugal
49. Argentina
50. Uruguay
52. Bahamas
53. Mexico
54. Costa Rica
60. Panama
87. Thailand
93. Belize

Any country with a ranking from 1 to 40 I would consider a first-world country with high levels of infrastructure. These countries are usually found in Western Europe and include the United States, Australia, New Zealand and the most developed countries in the world. These countries are also the most expensive to live in. Any country that has a ranking between 40 and 60 I would consider a developing country with a high income. In these countries you will see considerable poverty, but as a Western expat you will have access to first-world standards of healthcare if you can afford it. Crime will be prevalent, and but the cost of living will be affordable for someone subsisting on solely a state pension.

Countries ranked between 60 and 90 are quite poor, and in many cases will lack any strong infrastructure. That means most of that country's hospitals will be poor, and crime will be common. There is also a greater chance for instability and rioting. A country like Thailand will have some first world infrastructure in its biggest cities, but it will also suffer from high levels of crime and government instability. While these countries are very affordable, they are also very dangerous.

Countries with rankings over 100 typically are the poorest in the world and the most unstable. The Philippines (ranked 105) and Vietnam (ranked 116) are the most prominent examples of retirement destinations with rankings over 100. The former has periodic instability and high crime, while the latter lacks strong infrastructure and is quite poor as well. Countries with similar rankings tend to be extremely overpopulated.

Use HDI as another **tool** to analyze countries along with their respective levels of income when judging to see whether you could live in that country. The very best tool you can use to judge a country are your own eyes and ears through a visit on the ground. But HDI is the best tool that academics have come up with, though it has many flaws. The development of countries is a very complex thing. Different countries move forward differently, depending on their location in the world, the stability of their government, and the will of their own people to make more of themselves. Use HDI as a very general guideline and as a comparison to others to see what level of poverty you are willing to live with, in your search for a new home.

Credit default swap prices and the likelihood of sovereign default

One of the best ways to determine whether economic trouble is nearby for a country is to look at the price of **credit default swaps (CDS)** for a country's sovereign bond or debt. A CDS is a sort of insurance policy against the default of the bond. When the issuer of a bond defaults, if the bond owner also owns a CDS on the bond, the company that issued the CDS would pay him for his loss.

The **more expensive** the CDS is, the more likely the market and the insurer see the bond as likely to default. As of May 2010, the countries with the most expensive CDS were Venezuela, Argentina, and then Greece. The country with the cheapest CDS? The United States of America. The USA is normally viewed by global markets as the most economically stable country. Recent turmoil in the European Union proves this. If there is any currency you must bet on, bet on the U.S. dollar.

If you are a Westerner, particularly an American, you must realize that any country you move to will be less stable economically. Countries with high CDS prices are **the most likely to default**. A default results in (usually) an International Monetary Fund bailout, and severe cuts in government services. The reaction of the populace is almost always protests and possibly rioting. If you move to a country like Argentina, and Argentina's government defaults on its debt, or restructures its debt (which in many ways is simply another form of default) you can fully expect **turmoil** to ensue.

By turmoil I don't necessarily mean full revolution, though that is certainly possible. I mean what we have seen in Greece in 2010: massive rioting, burning buildings, and some deaths. These are more **common** occurrences in countries with fiscally irresponsible governments. Fiscally irresponsible governments are more likely to be found in the developing world, as well as in southern Europe.

For an expat moving to a more **affordable** country the old maxim applies: you get what you pay for. When you move to a country that is extremely affordable, like Argentina, Portugal, Spain, or Vietnam (all countries with high cost CDS for their sovereign debt), while you can expect to live a calm and peaceful existence most of the time, there is always a lurking **possibility** of civil unrest. The civil unrest occurs because the first thing a government does when it cannot pay off its creditors is to either tax its citizens more aggressively, or to cut services that they depend on.

The cutting of services will mean **furloughs** or outright **firing** of government employees. It will mean pension cuts for their own retirees (this won't affect you, obviously, as a foreigner), and it may mean hospital services will receive cuts. (This may very well affect you!) All in all, it leads to instability.

My point in all this is to hammer home the point that there is no such thing as a free lunch. Many countries irresponsibly allow their economies to run on credit. The Greek government literally lied in its accounting and told the European Union that its deficit was far lower than it actually was. The era of Greece living well beyond its means came to a **sudden** and **undignified** end. Retirees living there were caught in the middle.

Take into consideration the financial stability of the country you are thinking about moving to. By looking at CDS prices before you choose to move there, or at least keeping track of them as you live in your new country, you will have probably the **best** tool to measure your new country's immediate future. If things get rough, you may need to leave in a hurry, or at least prepare for a period of **austerity** and popular anger against the government.

Currency devaluation and what it might mean for you
One of the potential problems in moving abroad is the risk of currency devaluation. **Any country in the world** has the potential to have this problem, though it is far more likely to occur in the developing world

where fiscal discipline on the part of the local government is far less than in the developed world. That being said, even the most responsible countries have seen their currencies collapse and a default or devaluation on their debt obligations occur. **Iceland** in 2009 is the most obvious example.

When a country devalues its currency, it is essentially **printing more money** in order to pay its debts. Historically, that meant that the country would go into **hyperinflation** and the country's currency would become all but worthless. The most famous example that comes to mind is the **Weimar Republic,** which was the name of Germany's government before WWII. Germany printed more money to pay off its enormous debts to the other European powers and the United States, as a result of its losing the First World War. A more recent example is that of **Zimbabwe**. In both examples the governments felt compelled to print money to pay off enormous debts. Both efforts were **unsuccessful** and led to scenes of people pushing wheelbarrows filled with worthless currency in order to buy basic items.

Hyperinflation **destroys** the savings of everyone in the country. If the government creates a new currency to stem hyperinflation, the result **permanently** wipes out people's savings. This will obviously have an effect on not only the country's citizens, but residents, such as expats, as well.

In today's world, hyperinflation is a rarity. But it is still possible, as Zimbabwe has shown. For most countries under the threat of hyperinflation or default, there is an organization of last resort that will usually issue loans in **dollars** for a country to pay its debts. That organization is the **International Monetary Fund (IMF).**

Where to Live

The most recent example of a country defaulting on its debt is Iceland. Before the current financial crisis, Iceland was viewed by many as one of the best countries in the world to live in. Its high standard of living was due in large part to its financial sector, which made up a considerable part of the country's economy. The Icelandic financial sector became **indebted** to other financial institutions around the world, and when a **credit crunch** occurred, all of Iceland's banks were unable to pay their depositors or creditors.

The result was that Iceland's entire financial system collapsed. For our purposes, the experience of retail depositors in Iceland's banking system is important to look at. Virtually all accounts were **frozen**, and depositors were unable to get to their money. Many people from around the world had put their money in Icelandic banks because of the appearance of Iceland as a **stable** country with very high rates of interest on savings accounts. Now, with the credit crunch in full force, Iceland's bank accounts appeared to be a deal **too good to be true**.

Iceland's Krona overnight threatened to become worthless, and only an enormous bailout package from both the IMF and a large number of European nations saved the currency and Iceland's banking system. But for those who invested in Iceland and deposited in its banks, there were moments of doubt as to whether they would get everything they invested back.

Many Europeans had invested in Icelandic banks under programs such as **Icesave** which gave far higher than market-average interest rates for deposit accounts. Banks in the developing world **routinely** offer depositors higher than average interest rates in order to attract customers. **Never** put your money in these accounts. Banks abroad are rarely insured by their governments and if they fail, your money goes with them.

It is also a common con for a criminal to set up a sort of **Ponzi scheme** by creating a bank and then offering high interest rates on accounts. Allen Stanford, an American, founded a bank in the country of Antigua and Barbuda known as the Bank of Antigua. The bank offered customers too-good-to-be-true returns on their accounts, and when the market went into recession, depositors' money disappeared. Stanford is in prison now, but his customers' money is gone. Remember if it is **too good to be true it probably is**. Keep your money in banks back home that are guaranteed to return your money if they go under.

The best way to protect yourself from currency devaluation is to have most of your money **kept in a stable currency**. What currencies are stable? **The most stable currency in the world is the U.S. dollar, followed by the Euro, then the Japanese yen, and finally the Swiss franc, in that order.** My reasoning for this is that these are the most

popular currencies in descending order held by the world's various central banks as **currency reserves**. As of 2009, the U.S. dollar makes up approximately 61.5 per cent of the world's currency reserves. The dollar is so popular a currency with all of the world's governments that is known as the world's reserve currency. Many commodities are officially priced in dollars, most famously oil. The dollar's status as the world's reserve currency allows the U.S. to run up huge trade deficits indefinitely, and suffer few if any repercussions. Whether this can last forever is another story.

You will hear periodically that the dollar is on its way out, or that the Euro is going to take the lead. Many countries who dislike the United States' domination of world finance will occasionally make announcements that they are trying to find an alternative to holding huge sums of dollars in their central banks. **Ignore them**. They are just complaining, and nothing more. There is no currency on the horizon that has the backing of a powerful nation behind it to take the place of the dollar. For those Americans living abroad who are thinking of abandoning their own currency for another, think again. The **foreign exchange market (FX)** does the vast majority of its trading in one currency only, the U.S. dollar, to the tune of well over 80 per cent of trades. The market believes the dollar is the currency of choice. Shouldn't you?

While the Euro is growing in popularity, as of 2010, with the crisis surrounding Greece and that country's risk of default, you can see that the only true safe currency in the world is the almighty U.S. dollar. That is not to say that this will be the case forever. All empires fall, as do all reserve currencies. But until the Euro gives its Central Bank the same powers the United States' Federal Reserve has over its currency, you can expect periodic shocks to the value of the Euro.

That is not to say that the Euro is not a great currency to have your money in. I believe, based on the popularity of certain currencies as currency reserves, and the popularity of currencies traded, that there are about twelve currencies that a retiree can confidently store their money in. Those currencies are in descending order of safety: U.S. dollar, Euro, Japanese yen, Pound sterling, Swiss franc, Australian dollar, Canadian dollar, Swedish kroner, Hong Kong dollar, Norwegian krone, New Zealand dollar, Singapore dollar. The top six are very stable. All of these countries have shown pretty strong **fiscal responsibility** for decades. Yes, there are occasional bouts with inflation, but nothing unreasonable.

My advice for a retiree expat coming from the developed world and moving to the developing world is to keep the **bulk of your money** in your own currency at all times. Avoid putting substantial amounts of money in the local currency. Developing world currencies are **weak** and volatile and periodically become inflated and worthless. Having the bulk of your money in dollars, Euros, pounds etc. will keep your money far safer. While the currencies of the developed world can suffer from inflation as well, they are being managed by far more fiscally responsible leaders than those of the developing world.

However, if you are moving from one **developed** country to another for your retirement, you should **convert** as much of your portfolio as possible to your new home's currency. Why? If you have retired to France from the United States for instance, and are dependent on an investor portfolio that is primarily in dollars, if the dollar goes through a period of inflation your budget will be hit hard! That means replacing U.S. savings bonds, which as a retiree you should primarily be invested in, into various European bonds, primarily from the strongest and most stable economies in the Euro-zone: France and/or Germany.

In the long run, the Euro and the pound will always be stronger currencies than the dollar. The British and EU Central Banks have embarked on long-term strategies to make this so. That means that whether you are a citizen of those countries, or are moving into them, adjust your expenses accordingly. If you come from a weaker currency like the U.S. dollar, you will always find that your currency buys less in those countries than at home. I expect this to stay this way **indefinitely.** If there are dramatic changes in the way things work, expect them to be discussed in future editions!

Conversely, you can also expect countries with smaller economies, or countries that are poorer, to have currencies of less value. So expect a Mexican peso to be worth less than a dollar or Euro, and a Canadian dollar and an Australian dollar to be near parity with the U.S. dollar. Every central bank in the world wants to keep these exchange rates as constant as possible, because to do otherwise means to risk inflation.

Having a currency worth less is **not** a sign of a weak economy, nor is having a currency worth more a sign of a strong economy. It is simply the monetary policy of those respective countries. Budget for it, but **don't worry** too much about it. The relative values are **usually arbitrary**. Exchange rates are set by central banks and are kept as constant as possible to prevent inflation, the greatest fiscal fear of every government.

Is the Euro stable?

One of the big questions to come out of this most recent global financial crisis is the stability of the Euro. Several countries in the Eurozone, including Greece, Spain, and Ireland, face the prospect of defaulting on their debt. The Euro is seen by some as a mistake.

I believe the Euro is a stable currency. However, the governmental structure of the Euro makes it a **federal** system similar to the United States. How is that relevant to default? The United States has **never defaulted** on its foreign debt, that is, the money it owes to foreign creditors through bonds and other Treasury-backed securities. But the states and cities within the United States **regularly default**. Currently California and Colorado have or are considering renegotiating the pensions of their state government employees, which could certainly be considered a form of default.

European countries within the Eurozone are essentially **states**. Like states in America they issue their own bonds. But without the means to print their own currency, and because they are dependent on the currency of a European Central Bank like the Federal Reserve of the United States, they will be put into indebted positions like American states such as California,

Colorado etc. This means they will most likely default more often than they have in the past.

However, the European Union as a whole will be a **reliable** entity. This is just my opinion, but I believe it is an opinion backed up by historical fact. The EU is facing its worst financial crisis in its short history, yet the calls for it to be broken up are on the fringe. Europe will survive and move forward, but countries within it will either outright default, renegotiate their debts, and/or take severe **austerity** measures to attempt to combat their debts and balance budgets.

You as a potential retiree to Europe should be aware that the country you are in may be individually more unstable, but **collectively** Europe as a whole is safer. The financial instability that came from the Great Depression and in some ways led to Fascism I do not believe will return. But the price for that general stability will be more regional fiscal instability in Europe, as the American experience demonstrates.

Which currencies are vulnerable?

Because all currencies are no longer backed by a precious metal such as gold or silver, in a sense all currencies are vulnerable to declining in value or becoming worthless. But what makes a country's currency actually lose value? In my opinion the **fiscal policy** of a currency's government is in part to blame. Countries with easy access to credit and that have a history of balanced budgets are far less likely to default or to jeopardize the value of their currency.

According to the book *This Time is Different*, a landmark study of countries and their history of default, there are essentially two tiers of countries. There are countries that default periodically, and there are more evolved countries (almost always Western countries) that rarely if ever default. Currencies in the first group are not to be trusted.

What are the odds of default?

If you move to a developing country, the chances that that country will default at some point during your stay there are **very high.** Historically, almost every country in the world has defaulted on its foreign debt, and devalued its currency as a consequence. In fact, according to *This Time is Different*, only six countries have never defaulted on their foreign debt: the United States, New Zealand, Australia, Canada, Thailand and Denmark.

That is a very short list, and there are 185 other countries in the world. Developing countries default regularly, rarely going more than thirty years without a currency devaluation to pay off debts. When a country allows its financial sector to go unregulated and to borrow too much, or when a country's government itself borrows too much money, a default and devaluation is sure to follow. Developing countries will also default with far lower amounts of debt than developed countries. Countries like the United States can borrow far higher amounts of money in relation to GDP than a developing country can, with no fear of default. The market has no confidence in a poor country's ability to pay off debt, so interest rates on loans to poor countries are usually much higher than to rich countries.

All of this stresses the point that you should keep as much of your money in your **home currency** as possible, and keep it in banks in your home country. The more money you have in local currency, the more that will be wiped out when a devaluation occurs. If you have most of your money in your home currency, you will be largely unscathed when default comes.

This is also another reason **not to buy property abroad**. Buying property abroad is essentially converting a large part of your money that is in a stable currency, into an asset that is valued in an unstable currency. If there is a local default, you will not be able to sell your house to local buyers, and will only be able to find buyers who are foreign expats like you. You may not think this is a problem, but any time you are selling a property and have lost a large chunk of potential buyers, it can make selling a nightmare.

Dollar denominated currencies

Currently, there are **nine** countries and territories that use the dollar outside the United States and **three** countries and territories that use the Euro. Other countries maintain one-to-one convertibility between the dollar and their local currency. Developing countries have long struggled with having nearly worthless currencies in which foreign investors and creditors refuse to do business. Some countries have taken it upon themselves to adopt two of the strongest and most stable currencies in the world, the dollar and the Euro, in order to grow their economy and add stability.

In the interim, if you are a developing country and you adopt a stable currency like the dollar, you are doing a lot to convince your citizens to have confidence in your economy and financial institutions. However, there are many **risks** involved with adopting a foreign and more stable currency that you do not yourself **print**.

One of the biggest risks is that if the country that uses a foreign currency, or maintains strict convertibility, gets too deeply into debt, it will **default** and not be able to pay off creditors. This happened to Argentina in 2002. The then government of Argentina had convinced itself that linking one-to-one to the more fiscally responsible American economy would result in stability. However, the adoption of the dollar link only covered up the Argentine government's inability to control its excessive borrowing.

Where to Live

Below are the countries in the developing world that have adopted the Euro or the Dollar as their own currency.

Countries and territories that use the Euro outside the Euro-zone:

1. Akrotiri and Dhekelia
2. Kosovo
3. Montenegro

Countries and territories that use the U.S. dollar outside the United States (Retirement destinations are marked with asterisks)

1. British Virgin Islands*
2. East Timor
3. Ecuador*
4. El Salvador
5. Marshall Islands
6. Micronesia
7. Palau
8. Panama*
9. Turks and Caicos Islands*

Other countries have intermittently linked their currencies to the dollar and Euro through a **peg**. Below are the countries and territories currently pegging their currency to the dollar (popular retirement destinations are highlighted):

1. Aruba*
2. Bahamas*
3. Bahrain

4. Barbados*
5. Bermuda*
6. Cayman Islands*
7. China
8. Cuba
9. East Caribbean Dollar countries (Antigua and Barbuda, Dominica, Grenada, Saint Kitts and Nevis, Saint Lucia, Saint Vincent and the Grenadines, Anguilla, Montserrat)
10. Djibouti
11. Eritrea
12. Hong Kong
13. Macau
14. Kuwait (pegged to several currencies including the dollar)
15. Lebanon
16. Maldives
17. Oman
18. Netherland Antilles (Curacao and Bonaire)*
19. Qatar
20. Saudi Arabia
21. United Arab Emirates
22. Venezuela

Countries whose currencies are pegged to the Euro:

1. Benin
2. Burkina Faso
3. Bulgaria
4. Cote d'Ivoire (Ivory Coast)
5. Cape Verde
6. Comoros
7. Cameroon

8. Central African Republic
9. Chad
10. Republic of Congo
11. Denmark
12. Estonia
13. Equatorial Guinea
14. Gabon
15. Guinea Bissau
16. French Polynesia
17. Latvia
18. Lithuania
19. New Caledonia
20. Wallis and Futuna
21. Mali
22. Niger
23. Senegal
24. Togo

You will notice that much of the Caribbean is linked to other currencies. Recently the Cayman Islands, famous as a center of money laundering and as a tax haven, was told by the British government to start taxing its residents and those who conduct business there in order to raise money. The Caymans cannot print more money because of their peg, and because they do not have taxes cannot raise revenue that way. Instead their only source of money in a time of crisis is to beg the British government, their owner, for a loan. **Beware of tax havens and territories whose currencies are pegged to others**. What seems safe and stable can collapse at any moment.

The major risk in linking your currency to a stronger one is that if you fall deeply into debt and tax revenues fall because of a recession, you will be unable to pay your debts. A government in this position will then panic and cut services (government jobs, renegotiate pensions, cut government projects such as bridges and buildings etc.) and in a final step issue a new currency or declare that the current currency is worth a different value.

The people of the country react by protesting and rioting as their savings are destroyed. So don't fool yourself that you are moving to a more stable country because that country has adopted the dollar or the Euro. Catastrophe is certainly a possibility.

CHAPTER FOUR – VISAS

There are three basic ways an expatriate emigrates to another country. The first way is through **employment**, but as this book is written with retirees in mind we will only acknowledge that this is a method of residency and nothing more. The other two ways to reside in a country are by gaining some kind of **permanent residency** or by continually renewing a **tourist** or short term entry stamp on your passport.

As a citizen of a developed first world country such as the United States, UK or France, etc., you will have a passport that allows you temporary entrance (usually lasting 60-90 days, perhaps longer, perhaps shorter depending on the country) into almost all of the countries of the world. In many developing countries you can actually "reside" using this type of arrangement. However, residing this way means having to take a trip out of the country for a short period of time at the expiration of your legally allotted stay. After a short time outside your new retirement home you then return to have your passport stamped again. This arrangement is popularly known in the expat community as the **visa run.**

The "visa run"

When living in Dubai, I **did** a visa run a couple of times. I was between jobs and didn't have an employment visa at the time. Re-entering Dubai after a plane trip from Muscat, Oman, I came to Dubai customs and sweated out a brief wait until my passport was stamped. As I waited in line, I was sure I was going to not be let back in the country, or at a minimum arrested. I wasn't breaking the law, or was I? As I approached the customs agent, dressed in the traditional Gulf Arab dish-dash, I handed him my passport, and watched him gaze through it for what seemed like an eternity.

And then nothing happened. I was ushered straight through after my passport was quickly stamped. I had worried over **nothing**.

My point in all of this is to tell those of you who are nervous about such things to avoid doing the visa run. I am a **cautious** type. I don't like bending the rules too much. I know I wasn't doing anything illegal due to the prestige of holding an American passport, but all the same it **felt** illegal. If I could have received some sort of permanent residency that would make me feel comfortable about going through customs, I would have applied for it. Dubai, like most developing countries or territories, frequently changes its visa laws for various reasons. Western expats in Dubai live in fear that their residency will be revoked and they will be deported. It's an uncomfortable existence.

Visa runs are also next to impossible, and most likely illegal, in the developed world. As countries become wealthier and join the pantheon of developed nations, immigrants are attracted to work in those countries. Swamped with **illegal** immigration, a country will immediately crack down and impose stricter regulation of its borders. If you decide to reside in a developing country for your retirement, and live by doing visa runs, be warned that at any moment that country's laws can change and leave you stranded. The backwater developing country you moved to might be the next developed country with very strict immigration policies. Getting permanent residency will avoid this issue.

The other reason why you should aspire to hold some sort of permanent legal residence is that it will create a paperwork trail you can use to **prove** to your home country that you reside abroad and are legally avoiding **home taxation**. If you are an American citizen, and the IRS audits you, the legal documents or passport stamp you have that asserts that you are domiciled abroad will come in **very handy**. Visa runs will not be seen in the same light.

I have, for the sake of completeness, included visa run information in the visa requirements of various countries below. You will notice that only developing countries allow them. If you must do them, be cautious. Find out from other expats if they are still allowing them. Many expats feel that in some countries, such as the Philippines or Malaysia, that is too expensive to get a retirement visa, and that a visa run is a cheap alternative. You can rest assured that if the local government decides to change visa laws, the first group that will receive a **crackdown** will be the expats who commit visa runs. Don't say I didn't warn you.

Retirement visas

The only countries you should consider retiring to should be those with established "retirement visa" programs. These go by a variety of names, depending on the local language and other factors, but they usually require you to have an income stream from a source outside the country, and they may also require you to hold a certain amount of cash in a local bank account for a period of time. In this way you'll get a retirement visa.

The Financial Guide to Retiring Abroad

There are countries that require you to buy property, or set up a business within the country in order to get some kind of residency. I **do not recommend** moving to those countries. Examples that spring to mind are the Persian Gulf countries and Mauritius, as well as some developed countries. Countries like these make it difficult for all but the wealthiest expats to move in **because they don't want any more immigrants**. In developing countries with laws like these, their unique blend of xenophobia and demands for your money make moving there a risk. If you are wealthy enough that you don't mind losing half a million dollars on a very risky and volatile property market, or in setting up a business that will probably fail, ignore my warning. Otherwise, stay away. Even if you can afford to move there, these countries' severe restrictions on retirees mean that only a few expat retirees will be able to live there, and you might miss out on joining a community of men and women **your own age**.

Some countries that would otherwise make ideal retirement destinations, such as the United States (for foreigners), or New Zealand, either do not have retirement visas at all or require a substantial sum of money to be given to the local government to gain residency rights. The only feasible way to retire in these countries would be to use a **snowbird** model. I describe this later in the book. Countries with strict immigration policies do not cater to foreign retirees and only allow them if they can be **sponsored** by a relative or in some cases another close associate. If you have a child who has immigrated to one of these countries, then retiring to that country is a possibility. Oddly, it is actually easier to immigrate to countries like Australia, New Zealand and the United States as a **highly skilled worker** than as a retiree. Retirees contribute to the economy through taxes, while skilled workers take jobs away from citizens. But I don't make the rules.

Visa requirements

In this section I will detail the **up to date** retirement visa requirements for some of the most popular retirement destinations for expat retirees. Some countries welcome retirees with open arms, and others do not at all. Not surprisingly, it is developed countries that tend to have the toughest retirement restrictions for foreigners. **If you are a citizen of a European Union country moving to another European Union country does not require a visa**. It may, however, require some kind of permit to stay indefinitely, but these are usually mere formalities and are done so that you qualify for healthcare and other social services. You will note that I use the local currency when I talk about how much money is required to qualify for the various retirement visas. Currencies are constantly fluctuating in value, particularly in poorer countries, but visa requirements change much more slowly which is why the local currency is used. However, some countries will give the price of their visas in **U.S. dollars**, as that is the reserve currency of the world and an international standard.

You will also notice that more conservative countries, such as those in Latin America, will only allow a person to immigrate with a spouse or dependent, and not a boyfriend or girlfriend. For those who have not formalized their relationship with marriage, or for those who are gay, this might be an issue, and will most likely require two separate applications for immigration. While this means more of a hassle, the good news is that these countries typically have a very low bar to qualify for a retirement visa. If both members of an unmarried couple are receiving their state pensions, they will easily pass all the requirements for any of the developing countries listed below.

The requirements I have listed below are an effort to be exact. However, they are always changing, and though I will update this list with every new edition of this e-book, you can never be too sure that these are the exact requirements. The point of printing these requirements is **to give you an idea** of the restrictions and regulations of various countries. Some countries will make it quite easy for you retire there, some will make it difficult, and others will make it very extraordinarily expensive for you.

As an applicant, you must remember that you have **no rights**. You are a foreigner asking to become a permanent guest in a new country. Changes can be made arbitrarily to the requirements in your application. It may take weeks or months to process. You may be denied for no reason at all. If a country has a change of leadership and cracks down on immigration, it may become impossible to retire there. Some countries may be too expensive or restrictive for you to consider moving there. Use the list below as a guide, and not as the final word on the subject of retirement visas.

Australia: To qualify for a retirement visa to Australia, you must be 55 years or older. This visa is known as an **Investor Retirement (Subclass 405)** visa. The Australian government describes this visa as meant for "self funded retirees" which is a nice way of saying **rich people**. If you are retired and merely subsisting on a state pension, Australia is not for you. The visa is valid for **4 years,** whereupon it can be renewed. You are not allowed to bring dependents (children) with you, but you can bring a spouse or boyfriend/girlfriend. The requirements are as follows:

- There is a fee of AUD230 to process the application
- You must be sponsored by an Australian state or territory government agency
- You must have assets valued at least AUD750,000 (AUD500,000 if you plan to live in a rural part of Australia)

Visas

- You and your partner combined must have a net annual income of AUD65,000 (AUD50,000 if you plan to live in a rural part of Australia)
- You and your partner must purchase adequate health insurance as you will not be eligible for public healthcare
- You may work up to 20 hours per week legally, but no more than that
- You must make a **designated investment** into the state or territory which you have been sponsored of AUD750,000, **which are in addition to the assets you own in the above requirement** (this means starting a business or more likely buying local government bonds in that amount)
- You must pass a health examination (if you have tuberculosis you will not be able to move to Australia)
- You must be of good character (a criminal background check will be performed)
- You will not be able to get permanent residency or citizenship as long as you are under this visa
- You may leave and enter the country as many times as you like with this visa
- You can renew this visa every four years as long as you still qualify, but you must make an additional designated investment of AUD500,000 in a local state or territory, AUD200,000 if you are in a rural area. Income stream and health insurance requirements are the same, as well as character
- You may apply for **Retirement Visa subclass 410** which will allow you to stay an additional 10 years. This visa is more generous, but is only available to you after you have successfully applied and received an Investor Retirement visa

As you can see this is one of the most difficult countries to retire to. The investment requirements are essentially legal government bribes. Only the wealthiest of retirees could consider moving to Australia. A far more affordable alternative would be to merely purchase a property, and reside only six months out of the year (or however long your tourist visa will allow you to stay as a citizen of another developed country). You may apply at the nearest Australian consulate. **Please note, visa runs are illegal for this country and should not be tried.**

New Zealand: Like Australia, New Zealand has very strict retirement visa guidelines. Below are the most up-to-date requirements for a **Temporary Retirement Category** visa:

- There is a fee of NZD2600 to process your application
- You must be 65 or older
- You will need to afford comprehensive private health insurance at all times during your stay as you are not eligible for public health care
- You must invest NZD750,000 in New Zealand for a period of two years
- You must put an additional NZD500,000 in **maintenance funds** (these are the funds that show you have saved money for yourself and they can be kept in any bank account)
- You must show an annual income of NZD60,000
- You have to show that the maintenance funds and the investment funds are owned by you
- You must show that the investment funds are **unencumbered** (meaning that they are not a loan, that this is actually your money and no one else's), were earned legally, and can be transferred through the banking system

- Acceptable investments that the investment funds can be put into are: bonds issued by New Zealand or one of its local governments, bonds issued by a New Zealand company traded on the New Zealand Debt Securities Market (New Zealand's stock market), New Zealand firms with at least a credit rating of BBB- from a reputable credit agency such as Standard and Poor's, or equity in a New Zealand company
- You many **not** invest in a residential property development, or a deposit taking financial institution (any type of bank or financial services company)
- Your investment funds cannot be used personally

As in Australia, you must essentially be a millionaire to get a retirement visa in New Zealand. If you have children or a spouse in the country, they can sponsor you and you can get around these extremely difficult requirements. However, there are **tax benefits** to moving to New Zealand, which are discussed in the taxation section of this e-book. New Zealand is a **tax haven** for foreign residents, which will offset some of the expenses related to investing in the country. **Visa runs are illegal for this country, and should not be tried.**

Below are the second tier of countries in terms of difficulty to get a retirement visa. All of these countries are in Europe. If you are a citizen of a European Union country, or an EEA country, then you are allowed to reside in these countries permanently, but you may have to pay a nominal fee to reside beyond a certain period of time and to take advantage of various social services such as the government-sponsored healthcare.

The Financial Guide to Retiring Abroad

France: For EU and EEC citizens, France allows you to stay indefinitely, and make use of the country's various civil services including healthcare. Some fees may apply. For other Westerners including Americans and Canadians, France has established a retirement visa known as a **long stay visa**. The requirements for this visa are as follows:

- A passport valid for three more months longer than your stay (so valid for a year and three months to get the maximum length of this visa)
- Two copies of the long stay application form filled out and signed (these are available in English)
- Two passport-sized photographs
- An OFII form with only the first half filled out. Once you have been approved you will take the rest of the form to the nearest OFII office in France to have the remainder filled out
- Proof of full coverage medical insurance for your stay in France
- A note saying you will not work in France, signed by you and notarized
- A notarized deed of your property in France or a copy of your rental contract
- Bank statements for the last three months of all bank accounts including CDs, checking, savings etc. to show financial solvency
- Proof of pensions if any
- You must apply in person

All forms are available online at France's embassy for your country. You are not allowed to work with this visa. Of course, EU and EEC citizens may work if they wish. The requirements for this visa are not stringent **so long as you are a citizen of a Western nation**. Other nationalities, typically from the developing world, will take longer. For a western nation the requirements for this visa are very modest. You will notice that there is no exact monetary requirement for how much money you need in your account. It is up to the consulate/embassy to decide whether you have enough. The amount most likely changes periodically to keep with inflation. Payment for the application can be made by Visa or MasterCard.

Italy: For EU and EEC citizens moving to this country for retirement is very straightforward. You may be required to pay a nominal fee if you intend to stay longer than a few months, but this requirement is a mere formality. Many Europeans ignore it. For Westerners from other developed countries, the requirements for a retirement visa are stricter. You must attain an **Elective Residency** Visa or "Residenza Selettiva o Dimora". Below are the requirements:

- Visa application form filled out (you can get this from your nearest Italian consulate or embassy
- A passport valid for at least three more months beyond the date of your visa request
- One recent passport photograph
- Proof of financial support (social security, pension status etc.)
- Proof of housing in Italy(rental agreement, title to property in Italy)
- Police record (showing you do not have a criminal background)
- Proof of health insurance for you and your family

I want to briefly note that those of Italian descent can apply for Italian citizenship directly and not have to deal with any of the issues surrounding visas. Italy has a very liberal program of giving those of Italian descent citizenship, **even if they do not speak Italian or have never been to the country**. The program is too complex for me to go into in this book, but I make note of it to remind those who are Italian and are considering moving to Italy in retirement.

The Financial Guide to Retiring Abroad

Italy is famous for having a labyrinthine bureaucracy. The requirements above may have changed as of this e-book's publication, but the basics are probably similar. Remember, the true determinant of whether you will get this visa is the decision of the consulate official who reviews your paperwork. Other requirements may be made depending on you or depending on new and previously unknown regulations.

Spain: For EU and EEC citizens you can freely move to the country at any time. You may be required to pay a nominal fee if you intend to stay longer than a few months, but this requirement is a mere formality. Many Europeans ignore it. For Westerners from other developed countries, the requirements for a retirement visa are stricter.

- Proof of sufficient funds/financial means of support (how much will depend on the consulate officials and your application)
- A medical certificate or letter from a doctor stating that you are free from communicable diseases (this must be translated into Spanish)
- Fees of 81 – 100 dollars depending on your nationality (wealthier countries' citizens pay more)
- Two Schengen visa application forms filled out
- Two passport photos
- A passport valid for at least one more year
- If married or bringing children bring documents that prove relationship (marriage certificate, birth certificate etc.)
- Police record of residence from last five years showing criminal history
- All documents must be original and will not be returned
- Once visa is approved and you enter Spain you must report to a police department to have a residence card created for you
- Additional requirements may apply at discretion of consulate staff

Visas

As you can see, Spain has a straightforward set of requirements. Spain realizes that retirement tourism is a significant part of its economy and has made an effort to make its visa process easygoing.

The following countries are all in the developing world, and all have programs for retirees that are relatively easy to qualify for if you are a Westerner with a state pension (such as Social Security, etc.). Uruguay does not have a retirement visa, but gives permanent residency very easily and in such a way as to attract Western retirees.

Argentina: This visa is also known as a **private income** visa. You need the following to qualify:
- Your birth certificate
- A passport that is valid for at least one more year with one complete blank page for the visa to be stamped (the visa is large)
- Four passport photographs
- Evidence of income of at least 2500 Argentine pesos per month. This includes you and all dependents. A letter from your government showing how much your pension is will suffice
- Completion of an application form that is available online at Argentina's embassy website for your country, or at the embassy or consulate nearest you
- Marriage certificate for you and your spouse if married
- No criminal record affidavit, signed by you and your local police station
- US$100 processing fee
- Your dependent has all the same requirements (birth certificate, criminal record etc.), plus his or her own US$100 processing fee
- This visa is valid for one year, but can be renewed once a year indefinitely

The Financial Guide to Retiring Abroad

As in much of Latin America, it is quite easy for Westerners to immigrate and stay indefinitely. Argentina currently is suffering from somewhat severe inflation, making the income requirement for this visa truly miniscule. Of course, severe inflation has considerable drawbacks that have subjected Argentina to periodic economic turmoil and the inevitable accompanying street protests.

Brazil: Like many of its neighbors, Brazil has a formal retirement visa program. Below are the requirements for this visa:

- You must be over 50 to apply
- You must apply to your nearest consulate or embassy
- You need an authenticated copy of your passport. This means going to a notary and swearing that your passport is yours and giving this document along with your passport to the Brazilian consulate where you are applying. The consulate charges a small fee for this
- A certified copy of your birth certificate
- A certified copy of your marriage certificate (if married)
- A letter from your government saying you do not have a police record (Americans ask from FBI, Brits from Scotland Yard etc.) Check with your closest Brazilian consulate for the exact requirements
- Proof that you have lived near the Brazilian consulate for the past year
- A notarized letter from your pension plan. The consulate charges a small fee to process this
- A letter from your bank that states it is responsible for transferring your pension to a bank in Brazil. The consulate charges a small fee to process this letter
- Brazil reserves the right to add requirements as it deems fit

Visas

After you have filled out the applications and submitted the required documents you must wait until the visa is processed. Then you will be asked to come into the consulate to pay the final fees, which are modest. A small fine is applied if you miss your appointment. **This visa is permanent:** there is no need to reapply. If you leave Brazil for a period of more than **two** years, you will need to reapply again. Once you move to Brazil you must register with the nearest police station within 30 days of your arrival.

This visa is remarkably easy to get, and unlike that of many other countries on this list, does not require you to renew your status. You will note that there is no minimum amount required for the monthly pension payment, making this one of the most liberal retirement visas available.

Belize: This country is the easiest English-speaking country in the world to retire to as a foreigner. It is also one of the poorest countries to have a formal retirement visa program. Below are the requirements for the Belizean retirement visa:

- You must receive at least US$2000 per month through a pension or annuity
- If the pension is from a private company, the company must be at least 20 years old
- If the pension is from a private company, you must have a letter certifying that the company will send the pension payments to a qualified financial institution in Belize
- If the pension is from a private company, you need two bank references that the company will send the pension payment

- If the pension is from a private company, you need a letter from a CPA (or certified accountant of your home country) stating that the company is at least 20 years old, that the pension amount is at least
- US$2000 per month, and that the letter from the company that details this information is authentic
- You must pass a background check carried out by the Belizean Ministry of National Security
- You must be at least 45 years of age
- All dependents (children under 18, and spouse) are included in the visa application
- A birth certificate of the applicant and each dependent is required
- A copy of a medical examination and AIDS test should be included in an application
- You must supply four front facing passport photos with the application and four profile passport photos
- If married and spouse is a dependent, include a marriage certificate
- A police record issued no more than one month before visa application
- Copies of passport of applicant and all dependents that has been certified by a Notary Public (or your country's equivalent)
- The application fee is US$150 and is nonrefundable
- There is a program fee of US$1000 to the Belizean Tourism Board as well
- For a **Qualified Retired Person Residency Card** there is a US$200 fee
- Each dependent must pay an additional US$750 to be allowed into the program

Gaining a retirement visa gives the qualified applicant some special **incentives.** Below are the incentives:

- One imported personal vehicle will be exempted from duty and tax
- One imported airplane will be exempted from duty and tax
- One boat for personal use will be exempted from duty and tax
- If you sell your personal vehicle, airplane, boat or other duty free item you must pay all relevant taxes and fees

Like many countries that try to recruit retirees, Belize has no taxes for outside income. This visa is applied for only once.

Mexico: I am including Mexico in this part of the book for completeness' sake because it is the most popular foreign retirement destination for Americans and Canadians. It is, however, a **very** dangerous country and I do not recommend that anyone retire there at this time. I cannot in good conscience recommend to a retiree a country that has the world's most violent city (Ciudad Juarez). Mexico is one of the easiest countries in the world to retire to, so long as you can prove you have the necessary outside income. Below are the visa requirements for a **visitante rentista,** or retired income holder visa (FM-3).

- A passport that is valid for at least one more year
- Two passport photographs of your face in profile looking to the right
- Two passport photographs of your face in front view
- Proof of monthly income of at least US$1000.
- An application with your address in Mexico, when you plan to travel, your port of entry (border crossing, port, or airport landing)
- Immediate family members are also allowed to come, but the minimum income requirement will rise by 25% per family member

- Any household goods you are importing need to be listed in Spanish with a description of what they are. Electrical appliances must include name, brand, model and serial number
- To import any good will require the payment of a consular stamp that costs US$127.00. Once you have this stamp you can show it to a customs official and they will let you pass with your goods without forcing you to pay a tariff
- This visa is valid for one year, whereupon it can be renewed for an additional year
- After five years of living on this visa you can either renew for a sixth time, or apply for more permanent residency with an **FM-2 visa**
- You may apply for this visa while abroad at any Mexican consulate or embassy
- You are not allowed to work while holding this visa
- There is no age requirement for this visa

As in other developing countries in Latin America, getting a retirement visa is remarkably easy. Mexico caters to foreign retirees, particularly Americans and Canadians. The FM-3 is very easy to get, but you can never qualify for permanent residency for the years you have it. To qualify for permanent residency you need an FM-2 visa. The FM-2 visa is like the FM-3 but the requirements are more difficult. After renewing the FM-2 visa five times (over five years), you can qualify for permanent residency. Below are the FM-2 visa requirements.

- You must apply for the FM-2 visa while in Mexico, either with a tourist visa, or while on an FM-3 visa. You cannot apply for this visa abroad
- After holding the FM-2 visa for five years, you can become an "immigrante" or immigrant

Visas

- You cannot work legally on this visa
- The income requirements are similar to the FM-3 visa requirements, but change rapidly according to currency fluctuations, which is why they are not included here. The one difference is that if you are **married** the income requirement per month **doubles**
- There is no age requirement for this visa

Because the requirements of the FM-2 visa are more difficult and ever-changing, I recommend using a Mexican lawyer to qualify for it. The only benefit I can see of holding an FM-2 visa is that it allows you after five years to qualify for permanent residency and you don't have to go through the somewhat annoying process of re-applying for a visa. However, once you are a permanent resident, you are **liable for income taxes** like any other Mexican permanent resident or citizen. As a retiree you will never have to pay income taxes, and can live tax free on your foreign income. **Visa runs are possible and legal for this country (every 180 days for Western passport holders).**

Uruguay: There are no retirement visas for Uruguay. Instead, you must qualify for **permanent residency**, which is actually very easy to obtain and is structured in such a way that Western retirees such as yourself can easily obtain it. Below are the requirements for obtaining permanent residency.

- First you must qualify for a tourist visa and enter the country legally. For holders of Western passports (EU, USA, etc.) you don't need a tourist visa, and upon entering the country legally can begin to apply for permanent residency
- You must submit a **letter** in Uruguay to an immigration officer that contains: your first and last name, your place and date of birth,

your address and phone number in Uruguay, a photocopy of your passport with the Uruguay entry stamp on it, your reason for applying for permanent residency (retirement)

- Children or spouses must separately initiate permanent residency applications, but they can do this at any time, rather than having to wait for the household head to qualify
- You must have a foreign income of at least US$1500 per month
- You need to present one passport photo
- A **judicial certificate** (background check proving you're not a criminal). This certificate needs to be from the country where you have lived for the past **five** years. It must include your most recent address. You may request your criminal record from the INTERPOL office in Uruguay
- **Health certificate** issued by the Health Department of Uruguay (done in Uruguay to show you are of good health and not carrying a communicable disease like tuberculosis)
- You must come with an interpreter if you do not speak Spanish
- Once you have been accepted for permanent residency the Dirección Nacional de Migración (Directorate of Immigration) will contact the customs authority to allow you bring with you household furniture and appliances

Normally I would not advocate taking permanent residency status but Uruguay is that rare country that makes its status easily available. While this may seem very convenient, and it is, by forcing a foreigner to have permanent legal status in the country opens the possibility that a future Uruguayan government might impose restrictions or taxes on you. There is also the issue of legal liability, and while I am no expert on Uruguayan law, holding permanent residency status in a country usually gives that country the right to impose restrictions on you or prosecute you more rigorously than if you were just a tourist. Visa runs are possible here, and might be a more realistic alternative for some people, as Argentina is just across the river. Uruguay is probably the best country in Latin America to retire to, all things considered, but the fact that it lacks a formal retirement visa is something to think about.

Are visa runs possible? Yes, as noted, visa runs are possible, and are commonly done via Argentina.

Philippines: The Philippines, along with Thailand and Malaysia, are the only three Asian destinations with formal retirement visa programs. The **Special Resident Retiree's Visa** (SRRV) has several requirements, and unlike those of some of its Asian neighbors, has somewhat expensive requirements. Below are the requirements:

- You must be at least 35 years old
- If you are between 35 and 49 years of age you must deposit at least US$75,000 in a bank specified by the Philippine Retirement Authority
- If you are 50 years old and above you must deposit at least US$50,000 in a bank specified by the Philippine Retirement Authority
- You must have a passport that is valid for at least six months when beginning the application
- Notarized law enforcement document (local police department, government etc.) stating you do not have a criminal history
- Medical Examination Form No. 11 authorized by a doctor stating you are in good health
- If married you need to show your marriage certificate
- Any dependents must show original copies of birth certificate
- Fees are US$1400, US$300 for spouse/dependent
- 12 Passport photos

- Completion of PRA application form

For some, the prohibitive cost of the bank deposit will make many think twice about retiring to the Philippines. *Note: Many expats do visa runs, as these are legal with a Western passport.* In my opinion, if you are serious about retiring to this country, having a legitimate SRRV visa will go a long way towards relieving you of the burden of doing the visa run. If you decide that you simply cannot afford the SRRV, a tourist visa will give you 21 days in the country, and then a trip to the immigration office is required to renew. Currently you can renew every 59 days beyond this for up to 16 months. After that you have to fly out of the country and return to begin the process all over again.

Costa Rica: If you hold a passport from a Western developed country, you will not need a tourist visa. Costa Rica is quickly becoming the leading foreign retirement destination for Americans and Canadians due to Mexico's instability and high crime. It would not surprise me at all if this country were to become the most popular destination very soon. However, popular things have a nasty habit of becoming **expensive.** Costa Rica's residency requirements are rising in cost, and will continue to rise as foreigners pour in. The retirement visa is called a **pensionado (pensioner) visa**. Below are the requirements:

- You must show that you receive at least US$1000 per month from a company, government or institution (your government pension qualifies you) that acts as a lifetime pension plan
- A letter addressed to the Director of Migration stating why you wish to settle in Costa Rica. The letter must include your name, nationality, date of birth, occupation, full name and nationality of applicant's parents, address of residence in Costa Rica, phone number in Costa Rica, name of legal representative in Costa Rica (you will need to hire an immigration lawyer in the country),

which consulate or embassy where you will finalize the application, port of entry

- You must be outside the country when processing the application
- You must show your birth certificate
- A photocopy of your passport authenticated by a notary or local equivalent
- A certificate issued by your police department stating that you do not have a criminal record
- Your marriage certificate if married
- Two passport photographs
- All documents must be translated into Spanish by an official translator of the Costa Rican Ministry of Foreign Affairs
- After three years of qualifying for this visa, you can apply for permanent residency

Are visa runs possible? Yes, via airplane to any foreign destination.

Dominican Republic: The Dominican Republic does not have a formal retirement visa, but grants **permanent residency** to retirees who can prove that they are "solvent", i.e. being given a valid state pension. The following are the requirements for permanent residency in the DR:

- Birth certificate
- The application can be made in the country or outside it, but it is recommended that it be done outside the country
- Letter of application signed by the applicant or legal representative and addressed to the Consul or, in case the person is already in the DR, the Minister of Foreign Relations
- The letter of request can be issued by an individual or a company.

- If the application is filled out by an individual it should contain: individual's name, nationality, place of residence, and the activity to which the applicant is or will be dedicated in the country.
- If the application is filled out by a company, in addition to the data on the applicant, the request should be made on company stationery, and signed by the highest ranking officer of the company, indicating the position the applicant will hold.
- Form 509-Ref, duly completed and signed by the applicant, to be submitted with the other documents to the Consulate or Ministry of Foreign Relations if the person is already in the Dominican Republic.
- Certificate of Good Conduct issued in the jurisdiction of origin. If the beneficiary has been more than three months in the Dominican Republic, it needs to be issued by the competent local judicial authority.
- Medical Health Certificate. Issued in the jurisdiction of origin. If the applicant has been living more than three months in the Dominican Republic, a recent medical certificate should be presented, legalized by the Ministry of Public Health (SESPAS).
- Three front view 2"x2" photographs.
- Certificate of the Department of Migration with proof of the last entry of the person to the country and copy of the Tourist Card.
- Two photocopies of the applicant's complete passport.

Panama: Panama is trying to become the world's leading destination for retiree expats. They have created an unprecedented program of discounts for retirees, with discounts for pensioners on many different things including:
- 25% discounts on utility bills
- 25% discount on airline tickets
- 30% discount on bus, boat and train fares

Visas

- 20% discount on doctor's bills and 15% on hospital services if no insurance applies (i.e. if you pay out of pocket)
- 1% reduction on home mortgages for homes used for personal residence
- 15% off on dental and eye exams (if you pay out of pocket)
- 20% discount on bills for technical and professional services
- 10% discount on medicines (if you pay out of pocket)
- Tax exemption to import a new car every two years (a very good deal for an expat, and this is one of the rare times I would recommend you import a car if you absolutely must own one in the country)

Like some other Latin American countries, Panama offers a **pensionado** (pensioner) visa. The visa's requirements are quite easy for any Western retiree to fulfill.

- You only have to be **over the age of 18** to qualify for this visa
- You need a guaranteed pension of at least US$500 per month from a government or company (US$600 for a couple)
- You need proof of a clean police record
- You need a health certificate from a Panamanian doctor saying you are fit (making sure you don't have tuberculosis is the leading issue)
- The application is once only! You never need to renew it again

Panama is the leading country in the world in making efforts to attract retirees to live within its borders. You will also note that Panama uses the U.S. dollar as its currency, which makes things very easy for most expats, especially Americans. Because the retiree visa acts as the equivalent to permanent residency, I would not bother applying for any other type of visa. The pensionado visa also seeks to entice retirees to buy property with a 1% reduction on mortgages. I would suggest ignoring the incentive, and renting. That 1% reduction is undoubtedly built into a mortgage offer and will be taken up by fees on the part of the issuing lender.

Are visa runs possible? Yes.

Thailand: I am including Thailand in this book for completeness' sake, because it is one of world's most popular retirement destinations and the country has made a great effort to attract retirees. However, it is an extremely dangerous country that is currently undergoing a mild **revolution**. As I write this, protesters against the government known as **Red Shirts** are being shot to death on the streets of Bangkok after having taken over one of the wealthiest districts in the city. Thailand is well known for its periodic instability and political unrest. The murder rate for this country is also somewhat high. Westerners are occasionally targeted for thievery, rape and murder. Be warned, and consult your country's consular services as to whether the country is safe to move to. Currently most Western nations have warned their citizens **not to move or visit there.** Below are the requirements for the **Non-immigrant visa category O-A "long stay":**

- Applicant must be aged 50 or older
- You cannot work in Thailand with this visa
- Applicant cannot be prohibited from entering Thailand for any reason
- Cannot have a criminal record in Thailand or original country of residence
- Must have nationality or legal residence in country where application is submitted (must apply outside Thailand)
- Cannot have "prohibitive" diseases: leprosy, tuberculosis, any addiction to drugs, elephantiasis, third phase of syphilis

Visas

- A valid passport and two copies, must be valid for 18 more months upon application date
- A medical certificate showing you have none of the prohibitive diseases listed above
- Three passport photographs of you with light background not wearing a hat or glasses
- A bank statement or financial statement saying you have a deposit amount equal to 800,000 baht (the local currency) and a monthly income of 65,000 baht. Or you must show you have a deposit account and an income of 800,000 baht per month
- For the deposit account statement you must submit a letter of guarantee from the bank
- A letter of verification from a police or government agency saying you have no criminal record, and this verification cannot be more than three months old
- A marriage certificate is required if married

Thailand is one of the easier countries in Asia to retire to, and that makes sense considering its popularity as a retirement destination.

Malaysia: I have included Malaysia here because its government has created a retirement visa and is setting out to attract pensioners to live within its borders. Many are probably surprised that Malaysia is to be considered at all as a possible destination for retirees. Its neighbor, Thailand, is the popular retiree destination and takes the bulk of Western pensioners who move to Southeast Asia. Malaysia is also seen as a conservative country because it is mostly Muslim. However, I feel it is in many ways a superior destination to Thailand in that it is far more stable, wealthier, and multicultural. Of course that stability has a drawback: boredom.

The Financial Guide to Retiring Abroad

Below are the requirements for Malaysian retiree visa (known as the **Malaysia My Second Home, MM2H**):

- If you are **below the age of 50,** you must show at least an offshore income of RM10,000 per month and proof of RM500,000 of liquid assets (savings)
- If you are **above the age of 50** you must show at least an offshore income of RM10,000 per month and proof of RM350,000 of liquid assets (savings)
- If you purchase a property of RM1,000,000 or more you can qualify with smaller amounts of income and liquid assets
- Once you have these amounts you will be given a conditional approval letter

The conditional approval is only the first step. There is another set of requirements before final approval:

- If you are **below the age of 50,** you must deposit RM300,000 into a fixed deposit account (an approved Malaysian bank account)
- After a year you can withdraw RM150,000 only to purchase a house, pay medical expenses, or pay for a child's education in the country
- You must keep RM150,000 in the account throughout your stay in the country
- If you are **above the age of 50** you must deposit RM150,000 into a fixed deposit account OR show proof of government pension funds of RM10,000 per month
- After one year you may withdraw RM50,000 to pay for a house, pay for a child's educational expenses in Malaysia, or pay for medical expenses

Visas

- You must keep RM100,000 in the account throughout your stay in the country

Below are requirements for all applicants **regardless** of age:

- You need a health report from a clinic or hospital in Malaysia saying you are in reasonable health
- You must have medical insurance, however if you cannot qualify due to a health condition an exemption can be made
- There are two ways to apply for this visa. One is through an **agent** (there is a list of licensed agents at http://www.mm2h.gov.my), the other is **directly.** The licensed agents are private companies which may or may not be reliable, but could be faster. Caveat emptor

As Malaysia is an upper-middle-income country that is relatively stable and prosperous for the region, the requirements to reside there indefinitely are lengthy and more onerous than for other middle-income countries such as Mexico or Panama. Below are the requirements for **direct** applications for the MM2H visa:

- You will need a cover letter with your reasons for retiring to Malaysia
- You will need a resume detailing your education, work experiences, various skills
- A copy of the MM2H application form filled out (found on web at www.mm2h.gov.my
- Three copies of IM12 form (social visit pass) which is found at the same website address. All dependents have to complete this form separately
- Four color passport photographs per applicant

- Copy of passport pages with identification information. If you have renewed your passport in the last 12 months you must also bring a copy of your previous passport
- Letter from police authority stating you are not a criminal
- A self declaration that you and your dependents are healthy. The form for this can be found at the link above
- Your marriage certificate if married
- Certified copy of birth certificate
- If you have a disabled child above the age of 21 coming with you, you must bring a letter of confirmation from a medical practitioner (describing the child's condition)
- Certified copy of three months of bank statements
- Last three months of income statements if still employed
- A letter of authorization from you allowing Malaysia My Second Home program to verify your financial documents with the various financial institutions you have listed on your application
- All documents must be translated into Malay
- Dependents are defined as unmarried children aged 21 years or younger, and parents over the age of 60
- Each applicant and dependent must pay for a **security bond**. The bond must be made out to "KETUA PENGARAH IMIGRESEN MALAYSIA" and be stamped for RM10.00 by the Inland Revenue Board of Malaysia (sort of a personal security deposit)
- The security bond amount depends on what country you are from with a range from RM500-RM2100. The wealthier the country, the more you will have to pay, with Americans paying the most at RM2100, and Europeans generally paying around RM2000

The deposit with a Malaysian bank happens **after** you have arrived in the country and received a conditional approval of your application. Getting healthcare also happens after you have arrived in the country.

Visas

The MM2H visa lasts **ten** years. In order to renew you will need the following:

- A letter of intention to continue the program
- Copy of passport and original

To **terminate** your MM2H visa after you have been approved the following is needed:

- Letter of intention to terminate stay in Malaysia
- A letter authorizing the withdrawal of your fixed deposit amount addressed to the Ministry of Tourism
- Your original passport
- Original and copy of flight ticket out of the country
- I-card (if you were given one)
- You must apply in person at the Immigration Department
- After your Social Visit Pass has been canceled, you may go to the relevant bank and withdraw your fixed deposit amount

The requirements listed are considerable, but of all the countries in the developing world, Malaysia makes the greatest efforts to attract pensioners, with a website that is very professional and which even includes video testimonies of applicants.

Nicaragua: Below are the current visa requirements for Nicaragua. This country is rather new to the retirement visa game but has created rules that are easy for the average Western expat to fulfill, and has added incentives for expats. Below are the visa requirements:

- A copy of your birth certificate

- A copy of your passport
- You must be over the age of 45
- A letter from your personal physician stating you are of sound mind and in good health
- A letter from your local law enforcement agency or national agency stating you do not have any criminal convictions
- You must show proof that you receive at least US$400 per month from a government or private pension
- You may provide a list of household goods you are bringing with you in order to avoid tariffs and other restrictions

Like many other Latin American countries, Nicaragua offers a very straightforward retirement visa program for expats.

Other visa options

Some of the countries above have extremely restrictive requirements for retiring within their borders. In countries like Australia and New Zealand, you must be a millionaire in order to qualify. Other countries, such as the Philippines and Malaysia, require you to have saved a considerable sum of money to qualify, but by no means an insurmountable amount. For many, however, this is too much.

For most countries, there remains the option of permanent residency through marriage. In all of the countries whose visa requirements I have listed above, there are other visas that can be gained through the marriage of a citizen of that country. However, marrying a citizen of another country in order to gain permanent residency or citizenship **is a common illegal activity**. Developed countries will make every effort to review your application thoroughly and make sure that your marriage is **legitimate**. You can expect a jail sentence and/or **deportation** if you are found out.

You can also expect to never be allowed back into the country. Make sure you have a genuine relationship before proceeding.

Which countries?

Not every country is a good retirement destination. While the main reason a person retires abroad is to save money and improve his or her standard of living, there are some countries whose poverty and turmoil are simply too great for me to recommend.

There are three organizations that rank countries according to their wealth. For our purposes, I feel that the **World Bank's** list, which divides the countries of the world into four groups according to the **income produced by their economies,** is the most relevant.

High-income countries make up the developed world. These countries are by and large expensive to live in, but have low levels of crime and poverty, and high levels of technology and infrastructure. If you can afford to retire in any of these countries, I recommend doing so. The Persian Gulf nations are considered high-income, but their residency and socially repressive laws make retiring in those countries unfeasible. They are also not the most stable of governments. Popular retirement destinations in the high-income group include: **France, Italy, Spain, Australia, New Zealand, Cyprus, Israel, Bahamas, Barbados, St. Maarten, Cayman Islands, Netherland Antilles, Aruba, Bermuda, Croatia, Spain, Portugal and Greece.** To be included on this list means that the per capita income of your economy is US$11,906 or greater. It's safe to say that the higher the per capita income, the higher the cost of living.

Upper-middle-income countries have a per capita income between US$3586-US$11,906. These countries are typically found throughout Latin America, and in parts of Southeast Asia (Malaysia for instance).

The Financial Guide to Retiring Abroad

Popular retirement destinations in this group include: **Mexico, Argentina, Uruguay, Chile, Panama, Costa Rica, and Brazil.** Countries in this income bracket have far greater social and political issues than countries in the high income bracket. While some of these countries, like Uruguay and Chile, are hallmarks of stability and progress, other countries such as Mexico and Brazil suffer from **considerable crime** and poverty, in spite of the power of their respective economies. Expatriates will be drawn to these countries for their affordability, and for the excitement that goes hand in hand with dynamic, growing yet impoverished economies.

Lower-middle-income countries have a per capita income between US$976-US$3,855. These countries are sometimes found in Latin America, but mostly found in Asia, and sometimes found in Africa. Countries in this bracket are typically even more unstable and problem filled than countries in the two higher brackets. However, they are also extremely dynamic and very likely to experience substantial economic growth. Though they are not likely to be retirement destinations, **China and India,** are the two leading examples of countries of this type. However high rates of growth are not sustainable forever, and will either taper off, or drop sharply will follow.

Popular retirement destinations in this income bracket include: **Belize**, the **Philippines**, **Thailand**, and **Nicaragua.** You will typically find substantial levels of poverty, and possibly crime. Periodic severe instability is the norm. I recommend the higher income bands far more for safety's sake. Of course, the potential for saving money and making more of your budget is usually greater in these countries.

Low-income countries have a per capita income of US$975 or less. Poverty is endemic in these countries. Most such nations are found in sub-Saharan Africa and some parts of Asia. Popular retirement destinations in this income bracket include **Vietnam** and possibly **Cambodia**. At this point you are approaching Joseph Conrad/*Heart of Darkness* level of habitation. Vietnam is really the only country I can recommend in this income bracket. War and poverty are endemic in this income bracket, and there are several countries that are essentially broken and not expected to improve in any way for the foreseeable future. While you are certain to be able to live well for little money, you will also find a financial system that is completely corrupt, a local government uncaring about its citizens' needs, and substantial levels of crime.

Looking at a country's **average** income means that half the population earns this level or more, and half earns less. I view this as critical information. When you are assessing your retirement, you will determine how much income you will have from your investments and from your state pension. The higher your income is relative to the average income of a country is a key determiner as to how much wealthier you are to the average person in that country. The wealthier you are, the better you will live.

The risk, however, is that the wealthier you are, the more conspicuous you will be to the average person. While you should always budget yourself to live better than those around you, make sure you live a lifestyle that is not so **ostentatious** that you become a target for the average person's hatred.

Rural vs. City
One of the biggest decisions you will make when you move abroad is what type of environment you will live in. The two most distinct choices are city (urban) vs. countryside (rural). Both have considerable pros and cons.

The Financial Guide to Retiring Abroad

Rural areas will have considerable natural beauty, cheaper property (both for purchase and for rent) and will have **less crime**. However, they will lack many amenities and will be more boring to live in, unless you lead a very **physically active** lifestyle that includes hiking, water sports etc. In my opinion the biggest drawback of living in a rural area is the lack of access to adequate **hospitals and doctors**. Road networks in rural areas always lack the quality of roads in urban centers, and if you suffer a serious injury, or suffer a heart attack or stroke, you will lose valuable time getting to a doctor across poor roads and long distances.

The other issue with buying or renting a home in a rural area is that, while you save money, you will pay more in maintenance costs to keep up the property. Rural properties are larger and have more grounds to deal with, and the property will require more of your time and energy. In retirement, you may wish for something less **demanding**. Living in a rural area will also make it harder to gain internet access. **Satellite internet** can be purchased, but it is expensive. I explain more about this option on my section discussing internet connections.

Urban centers have the benefits of being close to hospitals, close to cultural activities, but also **close to crime**. They are also considerably more expensive to live in than in rural areas. They also are centers of **pollution**. For someone in poor health, with a condition that requires occasional hospitalization, urban centers may be the only choice.

A possible alternative that may be the best of both worlds is the **suburbs**. Suburban sprawl is not unique to the United States or to highly-developed countries. It is also a growing feature of the developing world. While the idea of suburbs might disgust the more sophisticated expat, their moderately-priced large and modern homes, coupled with their closeness to parks and hospitals, might make this the best choice for some.

CHAPTER FIVE – TAXES

One of the biggest factors to consider when choosing the country you wish to retire in is its effect on your income. For some odd reason, retirement guides that deal with moving abroad gloss over this issue or don't talk about it all. I feel a discussion about it is essential, and a crucial part of your decision to retire abroad.

While most countries (the United States is a sad exception) do not tax you while you live abroad, you will typically have to pay taxes in your new home abroad. However, **there are many exceptions to this rule**. Unless you are substantially wealthy, I strongly suggest you at least consider the benefits of moving to countries that have low or negligible taxation for **legal** foreign residents. In a section later in this chapter, I mark those countries that do not tax foreign income at all.

Tax havens

Tax havens are not just for rich people. There are plenty of countries that seek to attract middle class Western retirees and do not tax foreign income, namely your pension. While countries such as Lichtenstein and Monaco come to mind as the ideal destinations for the wealthy due to their tax free status, the cost of living in those places is far too high for most people. Uruguay, Panama and Nicaragua are far more sensible locations for those wishing to legally avoid excessive taxation in retirement.

Tax treaties and avoiding double taxation

One of the keys to living successfully abroad is avoiding **double taxation.** Double taxation is where you are responsible for the taxes of your home country, and also paying tax in your new residence abroad. If you are collecting a state pension, you will very likely have to pay taxes on it to your home country. You must therefore make sure that wherever you move has either a **tax treaty** with your home country, ensuring that you will not be taxed twice, or that your new country does not tax **foreign earned income,** particularly from pensions. Double taxation may make it impossible for you to live in many countries.

Fortunately, much of the world realizes that double taxation is an enormous issue for expats, and many countries have agreed to tax treaties allowing you to not be taxed a second time, **so long as you pay the taxes owed in your home country**. Some countries, however, have **not** signed tax treaties, either because they simply refuse to and have decided to tax anyone who lives in their country regardless of his or her status (**bad**), **or** they have decided not to sign a treaty because they are a **tax haven** (**good**).

Taxes

In short a retirement destination is tax-friendly if it:

- Has signed a tax treaty with your home country
- Is a tax haven
- Has passed a law that specifically says it will not tax foreign earned income (i.e. pensions)

Tax rates and tax incentives

In this section I've laid out the income tax rates of most of the countries considered popular retirement destinations. If a country does not tax foreign income, I make a note of it. Typically, developed countries tax income no matter what the source is. If the country you wish to retire to taxes foreign income, make sure that this country has a tax treaty with your home country or you will be forced into paying **double taxation**. You will also notice that many countries with easy retirement visa programs may not necessarily have low tax rates for foreign residents. Argentina, for example, taxes foreign income, though its retirement visa requirements are quite lax.

I have also listed below the various **tax incentives** expats enjoy. Western countries almost never offer tax incentives to expats, as they have no trouble attracting expat immigrants. Developing countries, particularly those in Latin America, have rolled out the red carpet for expats. Many tax incentives, however, involve the purchase of property, and I have not included them here. As I have stated before, I do not view the purchase of property as something that will save you money; rather, I view it as something that will **destroy** your net worth, particularly if you move to the developing world, where property values fluctuate rapidly. Tax incentives I include usually pertain to low or no taxes on food and medicine.

You will also notice that some countries with low income tax rates more than make up for it with high VAT (sales tax) rates. This can hurt a person more than an income tax rate can, because it affects your food, clothing, and day-to-day purchases. Take every type of taxation into account when moving abroad. Governments will lower income tax rates to please the voters, only to sneakily raise other sales taxes in order to get additional revenue. However, the fact that a country has a high sales tax doesn't **necessarily mean that goods are expensive**. It just means that a high percentage of the price of a good is taxed. Also note: taxes on **food, medicine** and other necessities are often much lower.

Most countries that have income taxes tax **progressively**. That means that the more money you earn, the more of your money you pay in income tax. It also means that income is divided into **bands,** with the highest band taxed at the highest rate. Some countries have an alternative tax system known as a **flat tax**. This means that regardless of income you simply pay a certain percentage in income tax. This is known as a **regressive** tax, as both poor people and rich people pay the same percentage of their income to the tax authorities, but the tax bite is much more likely to hurt poor people's ability to survive. I have marked those countries with asterisks which do not tax foreign income. These countries are generally in Latin America, and are making considerable efforts to attract Western retirees. Below is the information, with the range of tax and at what level the top band is:

Argentina: Argentina has a progressive income tax rate of 9-35% with the top band at ARS 120,001 or above. Foreign income is taxed. Sales tax (VAT) is 21%, however locally-grown food is taxed at a lower rate at 10.5%.

Taxes

Uruguay*: Uruguay has a progressive income tax rate of 0-25% with the top band at BPC 1200. BPC is a reference wage unit that is not the Uruguayan currency. One BPC is approximately US$1244 as of 2009, but this has probably changed somewhat since then. Foreign income is **NOT** taxed. Sales tax (VAT) is 22%, but essential goods like medicine are taxed at 10%.

Dominican Republic: The Dominican Republic has a progressive income tax rate of 0-25% with the top band at over DOP 658,367.01. Foreign income is taxed. Sales tax (VAT) is 16% but some products sold in supermarkets are taxed less.

Mexico: Mexico has a progressive income tax rate of 3-28% with the top band at 8,601.51MXP and above. Foreign income is taxed, **however you may receive a tax credit for any foreign tax paid**. This is particularly useful for Americans who are still liable for taxes while living abroad, and who make up the bulk of foreign retirees in Mexico. Sales tax (VAT) is 16%, however there is no sales tax on medicines and some key foods.

Panama*: Panama has a progressive income tax rate of 0-27% with the top band at US$30,000 or more. Foreign income is **NOT** taxed. Sales tax (VAT) is 5%. Food, medicine and medical services have **no tax.**

Belize*: Belize has a regressive flat tax rate of 25% for all income. Foreign income is **NOT** taxed. Sales tax (VAT) is 10%. Medicine, hotels and food are not taxed.

Bermuda*: There are no income taxes in Bermuda unless you conduct business in Bermuda. Foreign income is **NOT** taxed. There is no sales tax (VAT) in the country either.

The Financial Guide to Retiring Abroad

Bahamas*: There are no income taxes in the Bahamas unless you conduct business in the Bahamas. Foreign income is **NOT** taxed. There is no sales tax (VAT) in the country either.

Brazil: Brazil has a progressive income tax rate of 0-27.5% with the top band at BRL42,894. Foreign income is taxed if you are a Brazilian **resident**. A Brazilian resident, for retiree purposes, is someone who lives in Brazil more than 184 days of the year. Average sales tax (VAT) is 20% but varies from state to state. Food, medicine and other necessities are taxed at lower rates depending on the item.

Costa Rica*: Costa Rica has a progressive income tax rate of 0-15% with the top band at CRC879,000. Foreign sources of income are NOT taxed. Sales tax (VAT) is 13% and this is generally true for all purchases. Sales taxes are viewed by the government as making up for lower income taxes.

Ecuador: Ecuador has a progressive income tax rate of 0-25% with the top band at US$54,400 or more. Foreign income is taxed. Sales tax (VAT) is 12%, but taxes are lower for some necessities like food and medicine.

France: France has a progressive income tax rate of 0-40% with the top band at €69,500 or more. Foreign income is taxed. For those over the age of 65, there is an extra tax-free allowance of €2,266 if total income does not exceed €13,950 and of €1,133, if total income is between €13,950 and €22,500. **For expats**, you may be able to deduct your health insurance costs and other costs related to your pension. Contact a French lawyer or accountant for more information. Sales tax (VAT) is 19.6% but food, agricultural products, water, books, magazines, hotels and medicine have a 5.5% rate.

Taxes

Spain: Spain has a progressive income tax rate of 0-43% with the top band at €53,407 or more. Spain's tax rate depends somewhat on which state or region of the country you live in, but the difference between tax rates is marginal. Of all the countries in this book, Spain's tax rate is the highest. Foreign income is taxed, but Spain has tax treaties with most Western countries. Sales tax (VAT) is 16%. However, public services, medicine, and some food are exempt from tax.

Nicaragua*: Nicaragua has a regressive flat income tax rate of 15% for all income earned within the country. However, foreign income is **NOT taxed**. Sales tax (VAT) is 15%, but food and other necessities are taxed at a 5-6% rate.

Thailand: Thailand has a progressive income tax rate of 0-37%, with the top band at 4,000,001 baht or above. Foreign income is taxed. People over the age of 65 get an **exemption** on the first Baht 190,000. Normally the exemption is only for those earning Baht 150,000 or less. This amount is very small, and a Western expat will more than likely be earning far more than this through his or her pension. Sales tax (VAT) is 7%.

Australia: Australia has a progressive income tax rate of 0-45%, with the top band at AUD180,001 or more. Sales tax (VAT) is 10% generally.

New Zealand: New Zealand has a progressive income tax rate of 0-38% with the top band at NZ$70,001 or more. Sales tax (VAT) is 12.5% generally.

Malaysia: Malaysia has a progressive income tax rate of 0-27%, with the top band at RM250,000 or more. Sales tax (VAT) is between 5-10% depending on the item purchased.

Estate taxes

If there is one way to run into trouble after you're gone, it is to buy property or other significant investments in another country. While I cannot go into the ramifications of estate taxes in every country listed as an ideal retirement destination in this e-book, I can say that if you purchase property overseas, there is a significant **danger** of having to pay estate taxes on that property in order to transfer it to heirs.

If you die **intestate** (without a will) and you own property overseas the local laws will apply and those laws may not be to your liking. Some jurisdictions may favor children over your spouse, or vice versa. If you are remarried and your children would like your property, you can expect a protracted fight between parties. More developed countries tend to have far larger estate taxes than developing countries as well.

The goal is to avoid **complexity**. Owning property in several countries means dealing with several legal systems, and far more issues and problems. No one is intimately familiar with several legal systems at once, not even attorneys. Avoid unnecessary entanglements by keeping the majority of your estate in one country and writing a will that makes this apparent for jurisdictional purposes in the event of a potential lawsuit after you have died.

CHAPTER SIX – HOW TO RETIRE

In virtually no literature concerning retiring abroad do we see a discussion of **how to retire** or **when to retire.** It is generally assumed that you are wealthy, willing to spend a fortune on a new property, and that discussions about the financial aspects of retirement are too complex or simply unimportant. I have included this chapter to give you a rough overview of the basic rules to live by in order to manage your investor portfolio to supply you with the income you need to survive successfully overseas.

The key to successfully retiring

In general, there are two phases to saving towards your retirement. As soon as you are able to work or at least save, you are in your **accumulation phase.** When you retire, you enter your **income phase.** Accumulation is a sophisticated way of saying **saving.** That is, in order for you to successfully retire, you must save throughout your working life.

How much should you save? In general, you should save **at least 10% of your income** every year. More would be optimal. The more you save, the more likely you are able to teach yourself to live within your means and **not spend more than you make**. By far the greatest reason retirees are poor is because they neglected to save during their working lifetime. If you learn to live within your means when you are working, it will be easier to transition into a retirement lifestyle in which you can live off your savings comfortably and reliably.

When to retire

Traditionally a person retires when they are eligible for their state pension (Social Security in the United States, state pension in UK, etc.). I suggest this is probably the best time as well. For many retirees who have linked their retirement to a plan that is reliant on a portfolio of mostly equities and bonds, the **volatility** of global markets has meant that if the markets have experienced substantial losses, a person's retirement savings will be depleted. This problem is **magnified** when you consider that many people have made ill-advised investment decisions.

In decades past, a worker could expect to receive a small state pension that would then be supplemented by his or her company's private pension. Increasingly, companies around the world have decided that it would be cheaper to implement a scheme whereby workers control their own retirement plans. Instead of receiving a pension, workers would receive extra pay that they then could put into financial exchanges. What seemed to be a good idea at the time has been **disastrous** for many, particularly in countries like the United States and the United Kingdom.

For this reason, I believe that a retiree who has invested poorly for whatever reason should structure his retirement so that he retires when he is eligible for his regular government pension. In fact, I would budget **my**

day to day expenses around that pension. Such a pension is almost certainly guaranteed to be there for you. While there will always be sensationalist articles in the media about how governments won't be able to fund their citizens' retirements, I believe that governments will do all they can to do so. The most likely voters are elderly, and as a group they represent a strong voting bloc. Political leaders are loathe to offend them as a group. Even in Greece in 2010, when that country had difficulty paying government debt, the Greek leadership worked relentlessly to make sure its retirees were taken care of. Short of a complete collapse in government, I think your state pension is the **most secure** part of your portfolio. Treat it as such.

A note to EU citizens

If you decide to move abroad to a country outside the European Union or the United States, your pension **may be frozen**. That is, it will not keep pace with the rate of inflation. Instead it will be frozen at the level in effect at the time you moved abroad to these countries. This is the result of a decision by the European Court of Human Rights in March 2010. While the decision affects only British citizens, the Court uses precedence for its decisions, and if other countries in the EU raise the issue with their pensioners, you can bet that the Court will side with them.

This is a crucial issue to deal with. If you are moving to a country with a low cost of living and a weak currency, it is less pressing as an issue, but if you are moving to a developed country such as Australia or Canada, it could affect your budget considerably. If you combine this issue with the fact that your retirement might stretch into decades, you have the potential for disaster. Remember, there's always **Eastern Europe!**

What to invest in

For most people there are really only two classes of assets to invest in. Those two classes are stocks (sometimes known as equities), and bonds (debt issued by corporations and governments). In my opinion investing in anything else is **far too risky.** That means no futures, no REITs, no hedge funds, no precious metals, etc. Historically, every other asset class has been shown to be too risky, too volatile, and delivers too little in return.

So how does one invest in these two classes? **The only reasonable way to invest in them is to use index funds**. (Index funds are sometimes known as tracker funds outside the United States). Index funds are inexpensive, typically linked to companies with high quality service, and have been shown to outperform all other types of funds and almost all individual managers in returns over the long run.

What about actively-managed funds where a specific fund manager makes regular "picks" of assets he thinks will have the highest return? Study after academic study has shown that virtually all active fund managers are unable to accurately pick the right stocks or assets and deliver higher returns than index funds of comparable assets. What I mean by this is that an actively-managed fund of equities from the New York Stock Exchange will dramatically underperform an index fund that invests in the same exchange. **Markets are too efficient for anyone but a lucky few to be able to pick the right stocks at the right time.**

By efficient I mean that the price of an asset reacts too quickly for all but the most skilled to take advantage of it. If someone has found an underpriced stock and starts buying it up because they are convinced it will rise at some point, whatever piece of information that person had to make his decision will be known by everyone almost instantly. We live in an age of instantaneous communication. The internet, telephones, the media, etc., all have given everyone access to the same information to pick stocks. Knowing secrets to make stock-picking decisions is actually **illegal** and is known as insider trading. The playing field is too level.

What if I think I know someone who can pick stocks?

Chances are he has only beaten the market for a short period of time. This is a **common occurrence**. The problem is that he will almost certainly underperform the market's return (i.e. the index's return) **over time**. You must also remember that actively managed funds **are more expensive** than index funds. That means they have to dramatically outperform index funds in order to make up **for the higher fees you are paying**.

You might be asking at this point, what about Warren Buffett and people like him? The problem with investing with a Warren Buffett type is that you have no idea that this person is going to outperform the market **before they actually do it**. Can you time travel back to the 1950s, when Warren started investing, to take advantage of his market-beating abilities? Of course not. You can only take advantage of Warren Buffett now. As of this writing Buffett is 79 years old. There is no guarantee of how much longer he has to live. When he passes on, in all likelihood his company, Berkshire Hathaway, will be broken up. And your investment will be broken up as well. This is probably one of the best examples of the risks of **not diversifying.**

Diversify, diversify, diversify

What does it mean to diversify? Diversification means investing in several different asset classes that have little to do with each other, or at least behave **inversely** towards one another. Stocks and government bonds behave inversely towards one another in general. When stocks are up bonds go down, and vice versa. In this way, a person who invests in stocks and bonds has more diversification than a person invested solely in stocks or solely in bonds.

Index funds offer the greatest diversity, because they invest in an entire index. That means they invest in **every stock in an index** or every bond in an index. Such diversity has been shown to make for a far safer investment than investing in a small number of stocks.

Take the Dow Jones Industrial Average, an index representing American companies that are leaders in their respective industries. The companies that form the index are some of the world's largest in terms of market capitalization. When it was formed in 1896, 12 companies made up the original index. Only one, **General Electric** is still on it. The others have either merged, or become too small to continue to be part of the index. What I mean by this example is to show you that **stock picking**, even of the world's largest and supposedly safest companies, is still risky business. If you look at the DJIA today, you will see that only seven of the 30 companies that make up the index have been there for more than 30 years. The rest have all been added in recent years.

If you think the results from buying stock of some of the world's largest companies are risky, take a look at the survival rate of smaller companies. Better to buy the entire index and have it managed **passively** for the duration of your life. You can't go wrong.

The most important rule for investing

I've discussed that the only two assets worth investing in are stocks and bonds. And I've told you that the only investment vehicles you should use to invest in those two asset classes are **index funds**. But how much money should you put in a stock index fund and how much money should you put in a bond index fund?

How to Retire

The general rule of thumb is **your age in bonds**. This means that if you are thirty years old, 30 per cent of your asset allocation will be in a bond index; the remaining 70 per cent will be in a stock index. **Stocks are far more volatile than bonds.** The more stocks you have, the more your portfolio will go up and down. This is why it is generally recommended that the **older you are, the more bonds you should hold.** Bonds are less likely to decline in value; however, they will never return as much money as a portfolio weighted towards stocks.

As you approach retirement, holding too many stocks can become dangerous. If your retirement is approaching in only a few years, and the market has a sudden collapse, a portfolio made up mostly of stocks could see as much as a 30-90 per cent decline. The latter actually occurred at the beginning of the Great Depression. Such a loss would be catastrophic and would take **years** to recover from.

Because bonds, particularly developed country government-issued bonds, react inversely to stocks, the more of these you hold the better you will weather any downturns in the economy. Passively-managed bond indexes, like their stock index counterparts, have also been shown to wildly outperform actively-managed funds that invest in bonds. I recommend them highly.

OK, indexes: I got it, but which ones?

Because of the importance of diversification, when it comes to stock indexes, I recommend investing only in the largest stock markets possible. If you are British, invest in the broadest FTSE index possible. Americans of course, would invest in a broad index covering the various exchanges such as the New York Stock Exchange and NASDAQ together (Examples are indexes that follow the S&P 500 and the Wilshire 5000). Europeans should choose an index fund that best represents the European economy at large. Many index fund providers have European-centric index funds that comprise most if not all of the shares listed on the Frankfurt and Paris financial exchanges, giving an investor a very good representation of the European economy as a whole.

For bonds an investor should invest in a bond fund, preferably one that invests in **long term** bonds issued by their own government. If you are a citizen living in the European Union, I suggest German or French government bonds. Those two countries have the most stable, strongest and fiscally responsible governments. As their bonds pay out in Euros, either is fine. Check **credit default swap** prices on each to see which the safer bet is. Germany's bonds are usually safer than French bonds by a small margin.

I am not entirely convinced that buying corporate bonds is a good idea, but buying a bond index fund that only holds corporate bonds of the **highest** credit ratings alongside **highly rated government bonds** is a good idea. Generally when stocks crash, investors quickly buy bonds, but when the stocks really crash, they tend to only buy government bonds and sell corporate bonds of all kinds. **Never buy junk bonds** or bonds with poor credit ratings, no matter what their yields may be. It's just too risky. Bonds should be viewed as a refuge from stocks, not a speculative investment.

Retirement accounts

The biggest thing to take advantage of is a retirement account. In many developed countries governments give every citizen the option of saving their money in a **tax deferred** retirement account. In the United States these are known as IRAs, Roth IRAs, 401Ks etc.; in the UK there is the ISA. These are an essential part to successfully funding a comfortable retirement. I strongly suggest you take advantage of them at the earliest possible point in your career.

But what should you put in them? The best investment vehicle to put in a retirement account is typically what is taxed the heaviest in your country. In the United States, bonds are taxed far more heavily than stocks because interest (what bonds pay) is taxed more heavily than capital gains (the profits incurred from selling a stock). Check with a reputable accountant to make sure which is ideal. In my opinion putting commodities or other items that pay no interest or dividends to an owner are not worthy of being put in a retirement account and should be held outside in a standard taxable account.

The other benefit to making use of a retirement account is that many companies that offer them to their employees also offer to match whatever amount of money you put in up to a certain percentage of your salary. **Take full advantage of this**. Matching benefits can literally double your retirement nest egg. It is literally free money.

Transferring to a better portfolio
If you decide that your portfolio is filled with too risky investments and you wish to move into more index funds or perhaps a heavier bond allocation, be aware of **tax consequences** for such a move. Typically within a retirement account there are no tax issues when selling or buying investments. But outside of one there may be very steep consequences. Check with an accountant or a lawyer specializing in taxation before making any significant changes to your portfolio.

Early retirement
Any financial discussion about retirement should at least have a brief discussion about retiring early. I define "early" as retiring before you are eligible for your state pension. I personally know of no one who has retired early and lives a normal lifestyle. Instead, the people I know who

have retired early (and by retired I mean are healthy, not on some sort of disability payment) live **very frugally**.

Most of the people who say they are retired early, say in their 20s or 30s are **liars.** They are selling you some sort of investment or seminar, and they describe their current lifestyle as one of luxury and opulence. In order to get your attention, they describe their life before retirement as one of overwork and despair. These people are professional con artists, and you should ignore them. They tend to appear on late night advertisements on cable channels in the United States; most European countries have banned them. You can still see their websites online, however.

If they were telling the truth, they would not be on television hawking things. That in and of itself should be a red flag because it means they are **not retired**, but actually working, in this case working to steal your money. Retiring early is possible, but it requires an enormous effort, and it requires **extreme saving and permanent frugality**.

The key to retiring early, as I see it, is to save a substantial amount of money. This will require either a **windfall** of some kind such as an inheritance, or the sale of a valuable asset such as a paid off home or a company you owned. Or it will require a **high salary**, the bulk of which is not spent but saved for a period of several years. Again, depending on the amount you have saved, in all probability you will have to live an austere existence. Why? Because retiring early means that you will live for a much longer time than the normal retiree. Most people who retire are in their 60s, and with a life expectancy in the late 70s or early 80s, only need to save up for that period. Someone who retires earlier will have to save for a much longer period of life.

How to Retire

Another risk to retiring early is that you will fail to make contributions to your state pension. Most state pensions are linked to income contributions made over the entire period of your career through taxation. If you retire before you are **eligible** for your pension, or before you can receive your **full** pension, you will reduce the most **guaranteed** income in your portfolio. In my opinion it is an unnecessary risk. In general, retire later than sooner.

The biggest risk of following the advice of someone who advocates retiring early is that they typically will advise the use of **leverage** to buy stocks, or to **flip property**. Both acts are very risky, and entail the use of **borrowed** money. While one action involves stocks, and the other property, because both are extremely risky, they tend to work only in strong **bull markets**. To succeed they require substantial **luck** rather than skill. I advise against either as a strategy. Historically, American stock markets decline in one out of every three years. Property market rises and falls largely coincide with the larger rises and falls of equity markets. If your leveraged investment declines in value, not only will the money you invested be gone, but you will also be indebted to the financial institution that lent you money in the first place.

The smarter strategy is **patience**. Accumulate your portfolio through the magic of **compound interest**.

Compound interest: the surest way to wealth

Allegedly Benjamin Franklin called compound interest the **eighth wonder of the world**, while Albert Einstein called it "the world's greatest discovery". Benjamin Franklin made use of compound interest by willing US$4400 to the cities of Philadelphia and Boston in 1785 to collect interest for 200 years. By 1990 more than **two million** dollars had accumulated from this small sum in Philadelphia, and **five million** dollars from this amount in Boston.

Compound interest can work for you, and is the only surefire way to accumulate money throughout your life. If you can find a set of assets that produce income or rise in value over time, and you buy more and more of them throughout your career, through the magic of compound interest you can achieve financial independence.

The trick to making compound interest work is **saving**. If you do not consistently save throughout your life, you will be hard pressed to retire comfortably. Saving is the single biggest factor to having a successful retirement. In order to save you must live within your means, throughout your life. That means as little credit card debt as possible, and as little debt as possible **period**. Successful retirement is a state of mind, not just a mathematical construct.

A rule of thumb I use is to save **at least 10 per cent** of my income every year. Never any less than that, and often times more than that. By putting this chunk of money in relatively safe investments such as index funds, I allow my money to grow steadily over time.

Length of life

One of the key elements in planning your retirement should be an understanding of your potentially **long life**. Obviously, if you were to fall over dead tomorrow, any retirement planning you've done would be wasted. I would argue that you should plan your retirement with the belief that you might very well live well into your **nineties**.

Currently, all developed countries can expect their citizens to enjoy an average life expectancy of almost 78 years. In several developed countries, including Canada, France, Australia, Italy, Japan and Sweden, the average life expectancy is over the age of 80! If you slice into those statistics and view separate socio-economic classes such as females, the upper class, and the upper middle class, life expectancy rises even further. In general, **the wealthier and better educated you are, the longer you are going to live**, as you have access to a better diet, better healthcare, and a safer environment. Women, for various genetic and biological reasons, normally outlive men. Take all these factors into account when considering your lifespan.

You can also never underestimate what advances in medical technology will be available to you as you age. However, the poorer the country you immigrate to is, the less likely you will be to have access to such treatments.

My point in all this is that you should never underestimate how long you will live. Spending wisely, and living within your means should be done throughout your life, and throughout your retirement. Even if you have no plans to leave anything to your heirs, spending everything you have on a luxurious lifestyle could mean poverty in the last years of your life.

Investing for retirement is actually easy

There is a common misconception in investing. You are told by so-called financial professionals that investing is difficult and that you need a professional to help you. **The opposite is true**. Financial advisors almost always add little to no value to a portfolio. Instead, through high fees and bad advice they **subtract value**, at times dramatically so. Financial advisors wish to appear on the same levels as doctors, lawyers, engineers and accountants. They drive nice cars and live in big houses. They often have a three-letter acronym after their name like "CFA", "CFP" etc. These titles are in no way, shape or form as hard to get as MD, ESQ, or CPA, nor is oversight of financial planners as thorough as that of other professions.

You should manage your portfolio **by yourself**. In fact, **fire your financial planner** if you have one now. The only time I suggest dealing with a financial planner, if you absolutely cannot stand to look at numbers, is to use one on a **fee-only basis**. That way they have little to no control over your finances, and you can take or leave their advice.

Mutual Funds and ETFs

The best way to invest in indexes is to invest either in mutual funds or exchange traded funds (better known as ETFs). ETFs are essentially funds that are listed on a stock exchange like any other stock. You can buy them through any broker.

Mutual funds must be purchased through a mutual fund company. The largest fund companies in the world offer index funds. There's no need to be exotic in your choices; the largest companies also tend to offer the best index mutual funds.

Basically there is an ETF for every version of an index mutual fund. So which should you choose? I would suggest whichever you are more comfortable with. ETFs are usually cheaper than their respective mutual funds, but not by a great deal. If you purchase an ETF you also have to take into consideration the fees charged by brokers. These can be expensive, but there are usually plenty of options in this area so you can afford to be choosy.

The advantage of mutual funds over ETFs is that you gain access to the **support staff** of the mutual fund company. Brokers are not in the business of offering you 24 hour a day support for your account; they are in the business of buying and selling shares. The small additional expense of a mutual fund may be worth it in this regard. Many mutual fund companies now offer ETF versions of their funds as well, making the differences between both virtually moot.

I am biased in that I believe **Vanguard** to be the pre-eminent indexing mutual fund firm. I do not believe you need to make investing complex by hiring middlemen to buy funds for you or to make fund decisions for you. The beauty of the indexing approach is that you simply save money and don't worry about the ups and downs of the market. Over time, you will more than likely have accumulated considerable wealth. But you must be patient, and you must **avoid** being **tempted** into other investment vehicles.

Use a retirement calculator

How do you know when you are ready to retire? How do you know if you have saved enough for retirement? Do you know, based on how much you've saved, how much you can spend in retirement?

Google "retirement calculator" and dozens will come up. I recommend Firecalc.com. This website takes into account various changes in inflation over an almost 150-year period. It's in dollars and not other currencies, unfortunately. But the idea is a sound one: **you can calculate how much you can safely spend from your savings based on the past performance of stocks and bonds.** However, remember that past performance is not a guarantee. The future is inherently unpredictable.

No retirement calculator will be 100% accurate. It cannot predict the future. The Euro could collapse, the dollar could collapse, anything can happen. The longer you are retired, the more vulnerable you are to significant changes in the world's economy. A calculator gives you a very basic idea as to how much you can spend comfortably without depleting your savings.

Avoid debt like the plague

As you approach retirement, or if you are in retirement, I suggest you avoid debt whenever possible. Debt comes in many forms, but perhaps the most common is credit card debt. Credit cards routinely have interest rates above 10% which compounded annually can make a debt grow spectacularly. The interest rates on some credit card debt would make a loan shark blush.

For retirees on a fixed income, credit card debt represents a significant reduction in savings. Prioritize the paring down of credit card debt over other expenditures whenever possible. It's that damaging to your bottom line.

Where to learn about investing for retirement

The best place to go for retirement investment advice regardless of where you are located or what your nationality is, is the **Bogleheads** community located at www.bogleheads.org. This group of investors comes from all walks of life and many countries throughout the world. Don't be put off by the fact that most of the people at this forum are American; there is expert advice available for all nationalities, and expats living abroad routinely ask for financial advice on where to invest and where to save their money.

The forum is named after **John Bogle** one of the financial titans of the last forty years. John Bogle founded the **Vanguard Group**, the world's largest mutual fund company. Through his leadership, Vanguard became the first company to offer retail investors an index fund, Vanguard's **Vanguard VFINX** in 1976. The fund has gone on to become the world's largest with more than US$91.1 billion in assets under management. The fact that this fund has lasted this long, and manages this much money, is a tribute to the success of indexing and proof that this method of investing is better than any other for the average investor.

How to Retire

One of the mantras of the Bogleheads and many others who index invest is that a person should **avoid the noise**. That is, you should allocate money to your investments and let them do their work. Don't fall for advertisements or newspaper articles that are really advertisements in disguise, which argue that this or that investment is better and will "beat the market". Simply allocate according to your risk tolerance between equities and government backed long term bonds, and save regularly. When you retire you will have amassed a comfortable nest egg with which to live well in retirement anywhere in the world.

Chapter Seven – Healthcare

In my opinion, there's nothing more important to human happiness than **good health**. Quite simply, poor health prevents you from accomplishing your goals, will swallow up your time, and possibly leave you **destitute**. It's for these reasons that an in-depth discussion about healthcare is a necessity for any book about retirement and living abroad.

The importance of comprehensive healthcare insurance

The entire developed world, including the United States by 2014, offers comprehensive health insurance to all its citizens. Much of the developing world offers it as well, though it typically is lacking in quality compared with the healthcare offered by wealthier nations. However, as a foreign resident, you most likely will not qualify for this public plan. Instead you will be dependent on private insurance or your own money to pay for any healthcare.

Healthcare

As a retiree, in all likelihood you will find that you will be **making use** of local doctors more than someone of a younger age. It is because of this that comprehensive healthcare insurance is essential. Don't skimp on this area, even if paying out of pocket for healthcare is affordable for you. A critical injury, a long hospital stay, or extensive surgery all will mean thousands of dollars in expenses in you don't have insurance.

The basic rules for healthcare insurance

I am assuming that the audience for this book is made up of people from the developing world seeking to move overseas either to other developed countries, or to the developing world. This means that everyone reading this book has access to high quality healthcare in their home country if they require it. With that in mind, here are my basic rules for having healthcare when living abroad as a retiree:

- **Keep your home healthcare insurance, no matter what.** If you live abroad, and you come down with a chronic condition and your only healthcare is private, you might very well be dropped by your health insurance or not be given all the necessary treatments as the hospital or insurance company looks to save money. By keeping your home health insurance (which is probably run by the government, like Medicare or the NHS), you have the backup option of being flown out of the country and receiving free high-quality treatment. **Unregulated** private insurers are about profits first, treatment second. Private health insurance that you get abroad, particularly in the developing world, is unregulated, and may drop you if you become too expensive. So, if your home country's health insurance won't cover you if you do not keep up with payments, or will charge you more if you get back on their coverage as Medicare in the USA does, I strongly suggest you keep up with your payments. Remember the saying: **penny wise, pound foolish**.

- **Don't be afraid of a developed country's public healthcare system**. This section is written primarily for American readers. Many Americans are under the mistaken belief that government-issued healthcare is inferior or terrible, and they pay through the nose for additional private healthcare even when they are eligible for the local government healthcare. A key indicator of the effectiveness of a country's public healthcare is the country's life expectancy and infant mortality. Such statistics are readily available on the internet. The better the numbers, the more reliable the local healthcare has to be.

- **Look for high deductible, low premium plans**. In most countries, particularly those of the developing world, healthcare is inexpensive for basic things like doctor's visits, x-rays, and generic prescriptions. The more you pay out of pocket, the more reasonable your insurance costs will be. The higher the deductible, the lower the premium, which means the lower the monthly payment and less of an impact on your budget. If you are a healthy person, and rarely need to see a doctor, this could be to your advantage. I'm not advocating not seeing a doctor, I'm simply looking at this from a budgetary point of view. Insurance companies will view you as less of a health risk if they see that you are willing to pay more upfront. If you have a condition which requires regular medical attention, a low deductible plan is the better option, but you will pay for higher premiums.

Do I need medical evacuation insurance?

It's common for retirees and many expats living overseas to have health insurance with an option to evacuate them back to their home country for treatment in the event of a **serious** health emergency. The idea behind this

Healthcare

insurance is that if you are living in a poorer country, and you have something really bad happen to you such as a coma or a stroke, you will want the best treatment available and that means treatment back home, safely in the warm embrace of advanced Western medicine. I think there are times when this insurance is worth it, and I think there are times when it is **overkill**.

If you live in a developed country, I wouldn't bother, especially if you qualify for the publicly funded health insurance. The healthcare locally is world class, particularly in Western European countries such as France and Italy. In the developing world, you may want to consider purchasing it.

What a lot of expats don't understand is that their private healthcare, unless local laws say otherwise, **is not guaranteed**. That means that if you end up in a coma and your hospitalization is costing your health insurer a lot of money, they might drop you in the middle of treatment. An evacuation policy is a way out of this dilemma. By being evacuated back to your home country you can make use of your government-backed healthcare, which, as I warned before, you should do everything you can to keep.

Some might also consider holding evacuation insurance, and not getting local health insurance. That would mean paying for any local doctor visits **out of pocket**. I'm not sure if I can recommend this. As an American, I have seen firsthand what insurance companies are capable of if they are not ordered by the government to cover people under any circumstances.

If they can, they will drop you. I am a firm believer in having as many backups as is reasonable and possible. That means having good local health insurance, in addition to having an evacuation plan, and keeping your eligibility for your country's government-subsidized health insurance as well.

What about long term care insurance?

One of the biggest fears of an expat retiree is what he (or she) will do if he requires long term care at some point near the end of his life. **Alzheimer's disease** is probably one of the leading reasons for requiring full time assistance, and the facilities needed to adequately treat someone are expensive. In the developed world, an individual is usually placed in an **assisted care home** that is paid for by his nest egg or by his government. In the developing world, he is cared for by his extended family. For the expat, neither of these are likely options.

If you have retired to the developing world there are few if any suitable assisted care facilities. The only local solution is to hire a live-in nurse or assistant to care for you indefinitely. This will probably be far less expensive than comparable care back home, but the standard of care might not be as professional or regulated as it would be in an expat's home country. If the sick person does not speak the local language, then the problems associated with full time care are greatly magnified.

For male expats the most common solution is to have your wife take care of you. Sadly, most women will not have this option, as even if they are married that will be married to an older man who will die before them. I would guess that the issues associated with long term care are probably the **leading cause** of expats returning home to live out the rest of their days. The lifestyle associated with living abroad simply is unable to adequately deal with the problems associated with a terminally ill individual. Most expats either do **not plan** for this contingency, or do not care.

Healthcare

There are several preparations an individual can make to prepare for the worst and avoid the catastrophe associated with living abroad and requiring long term care:

1. Have regular contact with close relatives or friends. This is essential. If you begin to suffer dementia or the effects of illnesses associated with aging and you don't notice the effects yourself, your family will. They will be the ones to make the decision to move you back home or at least set up the assistance you need for treatment.
2. Maintain your home health insurance. Make sure you are eligible for long term care, either from a private or public provider. Your estate could be fined heavily if you return and demand care and have not kept up with payments.
3. Determine whether you are susceptible to various illnesses that could cause you to be put in long term care. Does your family have a history of Alzheimer's disease or stroke-related dementia etc? **If so, you should factor this in to your move abroad.**
4. Marry a local. This is more common of a solution than you think. It is also **fraught** with risks. The idea behind this is that in exchange for a monthly paycheck from your pension and investments, as well as love and companionship, you will get healthcare. The only way this can work is through mutual trust, and if you, the expat, think you can pull it off, then I say go for it. But the odds of something going wrong are substantial.

I do not view long term care insurance as a solution. It is not often available to expats, which doesn't make it helpful for someone living abroad. But even as backup insurance in the event you have to move back home it has problems:

1. It is never truly clear how much it covers.
2. You are dependent on the insurance company staying in business throughout your life. Insurance companies go bankrupt every day, leaving policy holders **shafted**.
3. It is largely unregulated, meaning policyholders can be dropped arbitrarily.

The challenge of getting long term care is one that we all face as citizens of developed countries. Our long life spans, and the fact that many Westerners are increasingly living alone in their later years means that this is a pressing issue. While care in a poorer country is relatively inexpensive, it is also lacking in quality. In parts of the world where there is high corruption and lack of government oversight, you run the risk of being abandoned if your estate falls behind in payments, or if no one trustworthy is around to care for you. At the end of the day the only real solution to this enormous issue is to plan ahead and have several backup plans in place if anything fails.

So which countries have the best healthcare systems?

The **World Health Organization (WHO)**, perhaps the world's leading health NGO, ranked in 2000 the healthcare systems of all of the world's countries. This ranking is the most recent, and it is unclear if the WHO will update the rankings, but the list remains the best comparative analysis of every country's ability to insure the health of its citizens. Below are the top ten countries:

1. France
2. Italy
3. San Marino
4. Andorra
5. Malta

Healthcare

6. Singapore
7. Spain
8. Oman
9. Austria
10. Japan
11. Norway
12. Portugal
32. Australia
41. New Zealand

As is typical with lists like these, we find that the leading countries all have very high cost of living and are mostly in the developed world. **France**, **Italy**, and **Spain** are all popular retiree destinations, while the rest of the countries are highly developed, and very expensive to live in. But it gives you a clearer picture as to where the countries with the best healthcare are. In the first 30 spots on the list, almost every country is located within Western Europe. The United States is ranked 37th.

Below are the rankings of some of the world's more popular retirement destinations in the developing world:

36. Costa Rica
47. Thailand
51. Dominican Republic
61. Mexico
65. Uruguay
71. Nicaragua
75. Argentina
95. Panama

The full list can be found at this website:
http://www.who.int/whr/2000/en/whr00_en.pdf

What causes a country to be ranked higher or lower? Basically, a country is ranked according to its efficacy at giving healthcare to all its people. That doesn't necessarily mean that a country is incapable of having good healthcare, it just means that only those who can afford it have any access. When moving to a country that ranks low on this WHO list, consider whether you will be able to afford top-tier healthcare there. If you can't, you might want to reconsider the country. You don't want to be on the bottom rung, with that country's poor.

How to find high-quality healthcare in a country

That is not to say that there aren't high quality healthcare facilities in the developing world. In countries such as Mexico, Panama, and Argentina, there exist world class facilities. **Joint Commission International** (JCI) is an American not-for-profit organization that accredits healthcare providers in the United States and throughout the world. **Accredited** hospitals and clinics are allegedly supposed to deliver the highest levels of healthcare to patients.

There is **skepticism** as to how **trustworthy** these accreditations are, as hospitals pay to have them done. I would discuss with your nearest embassy or consulate as to what hospitals they recommend for treatment in your new country. Below is a list of JCI-accredited hospitals found in a few countries that are popular retirement destinations for Western expats. You'll notice that larger countries with bigger economies have more hospitals. More hospitals means more spending on healthcare and more likelihood of being able to treat rare illnesses. Below are the countries with JCI accredited hospitals and the number of such hospitals each country has:

Healthcare

Mexico: nine hospitals and medical centers are accredited by JCI

Thailand: 11 hospitals and medical centers are accredited by JCI

Italy: 17 hospitals and medical centers are accredited by JCI

Portugal: three hospitals and medical centers are accredited by JCI

Costa Rica: three hospitals and medical centers are accredited by JCI

Spain: 17 hospitals and medical centers are accredited by JCI

Bahamas: One hospital is accredited by JCI

Brazil: 21 hospitals and medical centers are accredited by JCI

JCI also accredits hospitals throughout Western Europe and the United States. These accreditations should only be viewed as the beginning of your investigation into finding high-quality healthcare in the country you move to. You should ask expats about their experiences and if possible tour hospital facilities yourself.

Long term illnesses and being handicapped

Sadly, if you have a long term illness, or are handicapped, many countries will use that as an excuse **not to let you stay in their country**. Most of the countries listed in this e-book require you to submit a medical examination certificate of some sort. The two illnesses that countries fear the most are **tuberculosis** and **HIV**. If you have either of these two illnesses and are applying to retire to a country that requires a medical examination to qualify for residency, your application will most likely be **denied**.

If you have another health condition but it is not communicable (i.e. other people can't catch it) you have a better chance of your application being approved. However, your application's status is subject to the **whims** of the embassy/consulate/immigration department that is processing it. If they decide not to pass you, you are out of luck and will have no chance to appeal.

Bizarrely, it is the Western European countries and the United States that are less likely to discriminate against you if you have a medical condition such as HIV. The United States recently overturned its ban on immigrants and tourists with HIV, and Western European countries have no medical requirement to retire in their countries. However, if you cannot get a private health insurer to cover you, you will probably have failed a key requirement for your application, and you will be denied a visa.

Don't fear public healthcare in the developed world

Healthcare in the developed world is generally excellent. A recent ranking of Western healthcare systems by the Commonwealth Fund ranked several Western nations, including New Zealand, Australia, Canada, Germany, UK, and the Netherlands, as surpassing the United States in several different metrics. The study confirms the WHO's ranking of several years ago, and shows that the commitment of Western democracies to providing high quality health care to their citizens is still at the forefront of their responsibilities. Be confident in depending on them. If your private healthcare fails to provide for every service provided by local doctors in a

Western country, it is highly unlikely that treatment will be withheld as there are generally laws that prevent hospitals from stopping treatment on those who can't afford it.

Be afraid of public healthcare in parts of the developing world, if it even exists

Unfortunately, public healthcare in poor countries is generally, well, poor. If you depend on it, you can expect lengthy waiting times for treatment and poor treatment when you get it. Many doctors in the developing world are required to work a certain amount of hours for the public, but the real money and bulk of their income comes from their private treatments. In such conditions, a doctor will undoubtedly be more likely to work harder for a patient that pays him or her more. Those without private health insurance will likely miss out on the best treatment, or in the worst cases, will miss out on treatment altogether.

Such is the tradeoff for living in an affordable country. Your healthcare will not be guaranteed, and treatment may stop if you run out of money, with potentially lethal consequences. If you choose to live in the developing world, make sure you can afford private healthcare, and make sure your healthcare back home is up to date and paid for.

Vaccinations and malarial regimens

Probably the smartest way to avoid illness is to get vaccinated. Depending on which country you move to, however, you will need **different** vaccinations, as the diseases occurring in certain countries occur because of the climate and the environment. For instance, **malaria** is a disease carried by mosquitoes and found only in tropical and subtropical parts of the world. It is not found often in the developed world, because most of the developed world is in **cold and temperate** climates.

The Financial Guide to Retiring Abroad

If you move to a warmer and lusher climate, you can expect to face more and different diseases than you are used to. The world is a selfish place, and diseases that affect wealthier countries are the diseases that are cured first. It is for this reason that diseases that are unique to the developing world are a **constant and pervasive threat**, and there is often no cure in sight. Plan accordingly.

I have compiled below from a variety of pertinent medical sources a list of the most popular retirement destinations for expats, as well as the necessary vaccinations for those destinations. **Be sure to check with your doctor for the final say in determining whether these vaccinations are right for you. As I have no idea what your medical history is, I cannot have any idea whether you will have an adverse reaction to the vaccinations I have listed below. This is simply a general guide that serves as a starting point for your preparation to move abroad. Always check with your healthcare provider for final word on vaccinations for travel.**

1. The Caribbean

In general, the Caribbean is seen as an area where destination-specific vaccinations are not recommended. There are two **notable exceptions,** Haiti and the **Dominican Republic.** No one in their right mind would consider Haiti a retirement destination, but the Dominican Republic is very popular with expatriates. It is recommended that you begin a malaria regimen before going, particularly if you plan to visit rural areas.

For all other Caribbean destinations, a standard Hepatitis A, Typhoid, Tetanus, and Polio vaccination set should be done.

Healthcare

2. Central America

In **Mexico, Belize, Costa Rica, Nicaragua** and in many parts of **Panama** a malaria risk is present. Rural areas, particularly those with considerable jungle flora, have a considerable threat of malaria, urban centers less so. A standard Hepatitis A, Typhoid, Tetanus, and Polio vaccination set should be done as well.

3. South America

In rural parts of **Argentina,** particularly in the north of the country near the borders with Paraguay and Bolivia, there is a malarial risk. The two other popular retirement locales of **Uruguay and Chile** have no malarial risk. **Brazil** has some malarial risk in all areas, particularly in the Amazon basin and other rural locations. A **yellow fever** vaccination is also recommended for Brazil, particularly for visits to the Amazon and other rural areas. A standard Hepatitis A, Typhoid, Tetanus, and Polio vaccination set should be done as well.

4. East Asia

In some rural parts of **Thailand**, there is a malarial risk. Urban centers are malaria-free. **Vietnam** is a malarial risk in the entire country. A standard Hepatitis A, Typhoid, Tetanus, and Polio vaccination set should be done as well.

5. Oceania

Australia has no malarial risk, and only a Tetanus vaccine is recommended. **New Zealand** has no malarial risk, and only a Tetanus vaccine is recommended.

6. Europe

For those of you who wish to make Europe your retirement destination, no vaccinations are necessary other than Tetanus. A combination of developed-world status and a cold to temperate climate has made this part of the world safe from malaria and other tropical illnesses.

For the sake of space I have only included countries I feel are the most likely destinations for retirees. For further information consult www.traveldoctor.co.uk, or the U.S. State Department website. Consult your **primary care** physician for final advice.

Chapter Eight – Final Thoughts

Perhaps the most drastic and final act one can do as an expat is to renounce one's citizenship. The renunciation of citizenship is an uncommon act. It is usually done by those who either despise their home country, or who **are doing it to avoid excessive taxation**. The latter is typically the case with American citizens.

Renouncing your citizenship

As has been mentioned before, the United States is one of the few countries in the world, and the only one in the developed world, that taxes its citizens wherever they may be. This includes citizens who live abroad. However, as of 2010, Americans are able to exclude the first US$91,400 of their income (from all sources) from taxation. This amount increases every year according to the rate of inflation.

The Financial Guide to Retiring Abroad

According to a *New York Times* article from April 25, 2010, entitled "More American Expatriates Give Up Citizenship," the number of Americans renouncing their citizenship, though small, has been increasing dramatically in recent years. In 2009, 743 Americans renounced their citizenship through a straightforward procedure that was conducted through their local American consulate. The article hints that the main impetus behind the increased number of renunciations comes from **strict new bank account rules** whereby American bank account holders have been unable to keep bank accounts open as their bank in the United States closed their account in order to comply with new rules from the Departments of Treasury and Homeland Security. Though the United States has no per se law against having a U.S. bank account open if you live in a foreign country, banks err on the side of caution and will cancel your account if they feel you no longer have a valid address in the United States. The United States' paranoia concerning terrorism and its obsession with destroying tax havens has made living abroad difficult.

In my time abroad, I was fortunate to have my parent's address as my permanent "home address". This stresses the importance of having someone you trust, preferably a close relative, keep an address for you open. A P.O. Box will **not cut it.**

To overcome these difficulties, some will renounce their citizenship. In general I think renouncing your citizenship is a **bad idea.** If you hold **dual citizenship,** however, it might be **more palatable.** Not having citizenship makes you **stateless** and is a very bad proposition. It means you cannot count on any government to bail you out of trouble. It means if disaster strikes, no government will make an effort to evacuate you, or compensate you in any way. For all its flaws, and there are many, there are considerable benefits to keeping American citizenship, or any developed country's citizenship for that matter. I have also read about, but cannot

Final Thoughts

confirm, that many developed countries take a **dim view** of you when you renounce your citizenship. The film director Terry Gilliam renounced his American citizenship for British citizenship, and allegedly in order to **punish him**, he is now only allowed back into the United States for no more than 30 days a year. If this is true, it is yet another reason not to renounce your citizenship.

If you choose to renounce your citizenship, I strongly recommend that your back up citizenship be from **another developed country**. The entire world is divided into a giant caste system of sorts. Citizens of countries with passports from the United States, Canada, Western Europe and Japan as well as a few other smaller nations, are allowed easy access to virtually all of the world's countries. Poorer countries have severely restricted entry laws. **Henley & Partners**, a global consultancy that specializes in international residence and citizenship planning, publishes an annual **"Visa Restrictions Index."** This list is described as a global ranking of "countries according to travel freedom their citizens enjoy". Below is part of the 2009 edition of the list, with the number to the left of the country name signifying the ranking, and the number to the right of the country signifying the number of other countries that citizens of that named country can enter without a visa:

1 Denmark 157
2 Finland 156
2 Ireland 156
2 Portugal 156
3 Belgium 155
3 Germany 155
3 Sweden 155
3 United States 155
4 Canada 154

4 Italy 154

4 Japan 154

4 Luxembourg 154

4 Netherlands 154

4 Spain 154

5 Austria 153

5 Norway 153

6 France 152

6 United Kingdom 152

7 Australia 151

8 New Zealand 150

8 Singapore 150

9 Greece 149

9 Switzerland 149

20 Argentina 127

23 Brazil 122

24 Israel 118

27 Mexico 114

35 South Africa 88

53 Russian Federation 60

61 United Arab Emirates 52

70 Saudi Arabia 42

79 China 33

88 Iraq 23

89 Afghanistan 22

As you can see from the list, poor countries, particularly those whose citizens are Muslim, have severe visa restrictions. I will also add that due to the West's reaction to the events of 9/11, citizens of Muslim countries are usually required to check in with local police whenever they visit many of the higher ranked countries on this list.

Final Thoughts

You will also notice that the countries with a considerable number of retirees, such as Mexico, Argentina, Brazil and Israel, have considerably more visa restrictions than the countries of the developed world. No matter how much you fall in love with your new home, **keep your original citizenship**. You never know when you'll be planning another foreign holiday, or when you'll call upon the consular services of your home nation. There are also severe legal ramifications for having the citizenship of the country you live in as explained below.

Permanent residency and dual citizenship

While only a few brave expats will ever renounce their citizenship, many will take the opportunity to take permanent residency or even dual citizenship. There are many advantages to this, but also some disadvantages.

The most crucial benefit to taking on permanent residency or dual citizenship is that you can take advantage of many of the services that locals take for granted. If you have decided to retire to a developed country, you will have access to the health services of that country. As stated in the health section of this book, many countries' public health insurance systems are excellent, particularly in countries such as France and Italy. This could mean a cost savings of thousands of dollars a year. Of course if you are an EU citizen, there is really no point to taking advantage of what you already have. For Americans, Canadians and other Westerners who have decided to settle in the European Union, it could be worthwhile.

Having permanent residency/dual citizenship will also allow you to vote in local elections, and pass more easily through customs as you re-enter from abroad. These advantages, though, are somewhat **minor**. If you feel that you will become closer to the community where you make your home by taking on these new statuses, then you should do it.

You will notice, though, that is actually **difficult** to get citizenship in many parts of the developing world. While developed Western nations tend to publicly proclaim their dislike of the waves of immigrants settling in their countries, they have made great effort to assimilate these immigrants by putting them on the path to citizenship. Developing countries tend to see their immigrants as a necessary evil, or as a scourge to be deported, and make acquiring citizenship very difficult. Your retirement visa will be the only valid visa to have in those countries.

The biggest disadvantage to having permanent residency or dual citizenship is that it takes away some of the legal protections you might have as a foreigner. While the official word is that your government will allow local law to determine whether you are innocent or guilty of a crime, the truth is that if you are a Westerner living abroad, your government will scrutinize your case if you get into trouble with the local law, particularly if your case has a great deal of media attention. This is particularly true if you get into trouble with the law in the developing world and are a citizen of a wealthier country. And while no government will admit to paying ransoms/bribes to free its citizens under the guise of "we don't negotiate", every Western government will commit to backroom negotiations to free its citizens if they feel they have been imprisoned or accused unjustly.

Having dual citizenship gives the country you live in the right to say that they are administering justice to **one of their own**. Dual citizenship also puts you in a grayer area of the law. For many years few countries allowed the concept and they revoked the citizenship of their citizens if they took another country's passport. While that is no longer the case, no government looks upon dual citizenship very kindly. If you have ever applied to work for your government in a security-sensitive role, you will undoubtedly be asked if you have dual citizenship, as your loyalties may be seen as **divided**.

If you are living in a country with a retirement visa program, I suggest you remain happy with what you have, and put up with the minor inconveniences such a status entails. The issues stemming from a more permanent status are too great for any of the benefits you receive.

The snowbird alternative

Retiring overseas permanently is not for everyone. In fact it is **not for most**. For many retirees, the issues associated with moving overseas are too great. You may be separated from loved ones for too long, you may not be completely comfortable with the culture, and you may long to see your old home occasionally. There's absolutely nothing wrong with these feelings, and many of you can strike a balance between living overseas and living back at home.

Americans and Canadians call it being a **snowbird**. During the winters you move south to your exotic residence in the developing world, and during the summer you stay at your old home, conveniently missing out on any winter weather. There are many advantages and disadvantages to this setup.

In terms of healthcare costs, you may save significantly. **Travel health insurance** is far cheaper than expat health insurance. If you combine your travel insurance with the fact that as a retiree you have free healthcare at home (after age 65 for American citizens), you can see how you save significantly.

The Financial Guide to Retiring Abroad

Being a snowbird alleviates many of the issues associated with leaving loved ones for long periods of time, and if you miss your old home. However, if you decide to purchase a home, or sign a long term lease in your new country, you will have a dormant property for long periods of time. Even if you rent out your retirement property for considerable periods, because no one is managing it, you run the risk of your tenants **trashing** the place. I suggest a time share of some kind, or a house exchange if possible.

For some countries, being a "snowbird" is the only feasible alternative for many expats. Countries with restrictive immigration policies, such as the United States, Australia, and New Zealand, either do not have any sort of retirement visa (for example the United States) or require that an enormous amount of money be given to the local government for a period of time (Australia and New Zealand). In these countries it is realistic a foreign retiree that you will only be able to live there for several months a year, depending on the passport you hold. Typically this period is for six months if you are a Westerner.

The other advantage to being a snowbird is in the area of **taxation**. In many countries, you become eligible for taxes when you stay over a certain period of time, usually six months (check with a tax specialist in whatever country you relocate to for the exact period). Many countries do not have double taxation agreements with each other, and you may be liable for additional taxes if you stay for too long. The snowbird alternative is a way around this.

At the end of six months, you return to your home country. Obviously you will most likely move abroad to avoid cold winters, and take advantage of your home country's summers. The fact that Australia and New Zealand are below the equator means that the seasons are reversed, giving you an

Final Thoughts

ideal location to be a snowbird if you normally reside in the United States, Canada or Europe.

When to leave and come home for good

How do you know if and when you should leave your new country? You think you've found paradise. You have a beautiful home, the weather is perfect and the local cuisine is delectable. However, you notice substantial **unrest** in the streets. From what you can garner from other expatriates and from reading your home country's newspapers on the internet (the local newspapers are highly censored), your new country's government is corrupt, incompetent, and has angered many citizens.

While living in Bahrain, I noticed civil unrest on an almost weekly basis. It usually came in the form of small demonstrations that blocked roads with burning tires. It rarely became worse than that. Why didn't I leave? The Bahrainis I knew reassured me that this activity was "normal". My fellow expats didn't seem to care, either.

It all reminded me of that scene from the film *Godfather II*. Michael Corleone is in Cuba and discussing investing a substantial sum of money in the local economy. Earlier in the day he saw a Cuban rebel commit suicide with a hand grenade while being arrested. The resulting explosion killed a police captain. Michael is reassured that this is typical Cuban behavior. Later in the film, Fidel Castro comes to power.

There really is no clear solution. I suggest letting your nearest consulate or embassy know your location. I also suggest mapping out the quickest route from your home to the consulate in case of trouble.

I don't mean to sound paranoid. We live in an era of lessening unrest and growing wealth. However, corrupt poor countries have not learned to

197

distribute that wealth as equitably as others, leading to unrest and unhappiness. Understand the country you are moving to. Learn about its people.

Other expats can be both a great help and an obstacle

Expat guides for living and retiring abroad will portray your fellow expats as a source of information and assistance, and wonderful neighbors to boot. While all of that is certainly possible, and is usually the norm, not all expats are wonderful.

Expats are not necessarily like the people from home. They leave their home country for a variety of reasons, not all of which are good. Some don't fit in, others are running away from problems. That is not to say that every expat you meet is a potential serial killer or fugitive. On the contrary, the restrictions placed against criminals from moving abroad make it highly unlikely you will meet a criminal on the lam. There is an issue, however, with meeting what I call the typical **second chance expat.**

The second chance expat is someone who couldn't cut the mustard back home in his or her career, and views their new foreign home as a place where they can live cheaply, and work semi-competently, yet get paid well due to their status as a Westerner abroad; and a place where they can take advantage of the easygoing nightlife and the companionship it might provide. The second chance expat literally views living abroad as a second chance at life.

This type of expat appears more often in countries that are **poorer** and that have a reputation for an active **sex trade**. While this type of individual is certainly a down on his luck type (and they are typically male, though there is a female version), they are not all bad. The beauty of living abroad

Final Thoughts

is that even those who lack the wherewithal to prosper back home can bring their skillset to another country and add to it in some way.

As a retiree you can use this person as a guide to your new life abroad, so long as you view him or her as a friend rather than someone who is beneath you. While you may not enjoy this person's nightlife choices, he (or she) can point out the best affordable restaurants, who in the local government can help grease the wheels with the bureaucracy, and which are the best places to live cheaply. Never take anyone you meet for granted in your travels.

The other issue with living in expat communities is **gossip**. In my experience with the small number of Americans living in Dubai, I felt they tended to be **clannish** and distrustful of outsiders. They also held themselves apart from other expats, even those of similar cultures like Canadians! Expat communities tend to cluster around a social club of some sort, as well as certain neighborhoods.

There are tremendous benefits to associating with your country's expats. You will undoubtedly find people who know and understand your new country better than you. You may find contacts that can help you navigate government bureaucracies, and help you if you run into trouble.

One of my closest friends in the Persian Gulf was another American, and he was invaluable in assisting me in my occasional issues with local laws and customs. Without his help, I would have had a much rougher time. I met this person and his wife through an American business club in Dubai. The club introduced me to a few lifelong friends, and by avoiding the infighting and gossiping going on in the club, I was able to avoid many of the bad things associated with expat clubs.

In conclusion, look at expat clubs as a way to take a break from the local culture and to get a flavor of your home country. But don't get too involved in the activities of the club, or you may get swept up in the infighting and politics that are commonplace in any club.

Visit first

Wherever you decide to move, if you take only one piece of advice away from this book, follow this: **visit first**. And by visit I don't mean a week or two, I mean at least a month. Even more importantly, you should visit in different seasons in order to get a better picture of what you will have to deal with year round.

Here's a bit of strange advice: be sure to be in the country when a storm hits. In drier countries where rainfall is rare, the average person is unused to wet weather. Mudslides occur, people wreck more on the roads, and no one has an umbrella. When I was growing up in Los Angeles, this was a yearly occurrence, and the roads became wet and dangerous. In dry climates oils trapped in asphalt will rise to the surface of the roads during rainstorms and make the roads even more slick and dangerous.

Have an escape plan

As I have discussed before, a retiree should always keep open the option of leaving his home at a moment's notice. While stability in most countries occurs more often than turmoil, the poorer the country you live in, the more likely you will see:

- Street demonstrations, particularly against the government
- Intense poverty and unhappiness on the part of the poorest
- Rampant crime, including burglary and murder
- Enormous inequities in wealth, with an upper class that cares little about its fellow citizens

Final Thoughts

- An incompetent government that does little for its people and rewards only the wealthiest of its citizens
- A despairing and lazy local population that is fed up and pessimistic about the future
- Infrastructure in need of repair

All these things are factors in turmoil and societal breakdown. However, none of them is enough to result in your needing to leave the country. So when is it apparent that a revolution is around the corner?

The telltale sign of a revolution is the **massive street protest**. I'm not talking about five hundred college kids protesting in front of the university library: I mean **half a million to a million** everyday people protesting vigorously in front of the main government offices, particularly the President/Prime Minister/Emperor's palace whatever that may be called.

Revolutions almost always occur when the average people from all around the country, even the countryside, are protesting. When you see these people protesting, you know the end is near. Professional protesters such as students, hip urban young people, union professionals, these groups protest regularly. But there are never enough of them to make a difference. The army, which protects the leadership, is made up of working-class people and the rural poor. If the army is forced to fire on its own kind, it will lay down its arms and let the revolution commence. If the army is ordered to shoot students, young people, etc., it will happily do so. This is exactly what occurred in 2009 in **Iran** and is the key reason why that revolution failed.

Some countries are culturally more inclined to protest and have street demonstrations, such as **Argentina** and **France**. But these demonstrations almost always mean nothing. They never are representative of the whole of the country, and are done just to get a slightly larger handout or tax break from the government. So don't be worried. But if you see massive demonstrations in those countries lasting weeks, with the army facing off against them, then you should be panicking.

Evacuation

There may come a moment in your time abroad where you will have to leave because the country around you is falling apart, and your continued stay in the country might lead to your being killed. Frequently in times like this the best thing to do is to head to your nearest consulate or embassy. The embassy will have **well armed** security staff that are trained for eventualities such as the evacuation of citizens and staff living in the country.

If things erupt into full rebellion, get to the embassy or consulate as fast as possible. They will figure out how to get you out. In all likelihood you will be allowed to leave under **ceasefire** conditions. The rebels won't want to create a diplomatic incident by shooting embassy staff.

What they will do is shoot people who are acting **suspiciously,** trying to ram through barriers, or trying to sneak out for whatever reason. If you do this, they will most likely think you are one of their former political leaders trying to **elude punishment** for various crimes, and they will try to kill you. Do not be this person. Go to the embassy and hope for the best.

There is however, the possibility of an **Iran** scenario. In 1978 and 1979, Iran overthrew the Shah and instituted a theocracy that is in power to this day. That group purposely took over the U.S. embassy and held everyone there hostage for 444 days. No other embassies were taken over. In that case, the United States was seen by the new government as the protector and benefactor of the Shah.

Final Thoughts

Generally, if you are a citizen of a Western country and you make it into the embassy, you will be safe. However, in the case of the United States and to a lesser extent Britain and France, occasionally the local people will view these countries as allies of the old government that has just been overthrown. The U.S., Britain and France still maintain influence well beyond their borders, and are despised by many abroad for this reason. In countries where this influence is seen as non-existent, if you are a citizen of the U.S., Britain or France, you are probably safe. In other countries, particularly in the Middle East, not so much. Tread more carefully if you have these passports. Many parts of Latin America also view the United States with some hostility, and as having too great an influence in the region.

If a violent uprising is occurring and the local government is toppled, the rebels may be looking for foreigners to **hold hostage** in order to secure ransom and/or credibility. When rebels overthrow a government, the last act of that government is frequently to **loot the country.** That means taking foreign currency, namely U.S. dollars and Euros, as well as whatever gold reserves there may be. The new government that comes to power has a severe dilemma. They must secure foreign currency and gold in order to pay debts and to make sure that their own currency is not **worthless,** as currencies usually collapse when a government is overthrown. Foreign hostages are usually held for ransom and to get dollars from a foreign power, usually the United States.

Rest assured though: You are worth more alive than dead. You are worth money and political prestige as a passport holder of a Western country. If the locals wanted you dead, you'd have no chance for escape. If you are captured, it's highly likely that you are being kept around for a reason.

The Best Places to Retire

It's only natural that I list the best places to retire, as so many other retirement guides have. Unlike other listmakers, I take into account the cost of living, taxes and financial stability over other factors such as weather and cuisine. Countries that are unstable due to crime or politics, like as Mexico and Thailand, have not been included, but may find their way onto the list in future editions if they can recover their stability.

Without further ado here is my top ten list of retirement locations:

1. **Uruguay**. It is one of the cheapest places on earth. It gives people permanent residency very easily. It does not tax foreign income. And if you get bored, you can easily spend the day in Buenos Aires, which is just across the river.
2. **France**. You have affordable access to one of the best medical systems in the world, if not the best. However, it is probably the most expensive retirement location listed in this book. You will most likely live in a rural location if you move there. You also have easy access to the rest of Europe via train or plane.
3. **Panama**. It is relatively stable. It uses the dollar, which prevents the instability associated with having its own currency, and makes it very affordable for Western expats who either use the dollar or use a more valuable currency. Its healthcare system however leaves a lot to be desired.
4. **Costa Rica**. It is the most politically stable country in Latin America. It is relatively economically stable and prosperous. It is not as cheap as its neighbors and is getting more expensive by the day. Its medical systems are decent.
5. **Italy**. In many places, particularly in the south of the country, it is relatively affordable, particularly compared to

France. Its medical system leaves much to be desired, but is cheap and expats can access it relatively easily. You are close to the whole of Europe.

6. **Spain**. It is the most popular retirement destination in Europe, and rural areas are very affordable. But it's not as cheap as Portugal, or even rural southern Italy. Healthcare is decent quality, and English-speaking expats will easily find communities that share their language.

7. **United States**. It is the most affordable developed country, particularly in rural areas, but even in some cities such as Dallas and Raleigh. Its healthcare system is fabulous, **if you can afford it**. It is very difficult to get permanent residency here, and there are no retirement visas.

8. **Malaysia**. It is affordable, and is a prosperous developing country. It is much more **stable** than its neighbors Indonesia and Thailand. Healthcare is of a decent quality. Its Muslim government is intolerant of homosexuality and risqué behavior, which prevents it from being higher on this list. Also, retirement visas require a lot of paperwork in comparison with other destinations on this list.

9. **Argentina.** It is very affordable. Healthcare is cheap and decent. Foreign income is taxed, which hurts its status as a retirement destination. It is very easy to retire here from a visa standpoint. It is notoriously unstable economically, and a default is just around the corner.

10. **Nicaragua**. It is dirt cheap to live here. However, you get what you pay for to some extent. There is a great deal of poverty, and the country's infrastructure is not the best. Healthcare is cheap but its quality remains questionable.

The Financial Guide to Retiring Abroad

For more information on the financial aspects of being an expat and for access to my daily thoughts, visit my blog at **www.expatinvesting.org**. You can email me any questions you have about this book or about being an expat through the site as well. I hope you've enjoyed reading this book as much as I've enjoyed writing it, and I hope it gives you the insight necessary to live successfully in retirement in whatever country you choose.

Index

disabled, 75, 76, 140

Djibouti, 108

dollar, 9, 24, 27, 40, 45, 52, 55, 82, 89, 90, 96, 98, 100, 101, 102, 106, 107, 108, 110, 114, 115, 122, 135, 165, 169, 173, 191, 201, 202

Dominica, 108

Dominican Republic, 72, 89, 133, 134, 151, 179, 184

double taxation, 148, 149, 194

Dow Jones Industrial Average, 160

driving, 34, 36, 40, 41, 42, 43, 44, 79

drugs, 27, 64, 65, 66, 67, 136

Dubai, 19, 20, 45, 51, 57, 64, 93, 112, 197, 216

earthquake, 11, 33, 34

East Asia, 14, 70, 185

economic growth, 43, 47, 88, 144

economic history, 91

Economist, 85, 86

Ecuador, 69, 72, 89, 107, 152

El Salvador, 107

Elective Residency Visa, 121

Environmental Performance Index, 92

Equatorial Guinea, 109

Eritrea, 108

estate taxes, 154

Estonia, 109

Euro, 36, 89, 100, 101, 102, 103, 106, 107, 108, 110, 169

Europe, 9, 12, 13, 14, 15, 17, 27, 52, 55, 58, 64, 69, 74, 75, 80, 81, 89, 92, 94, 96, 97, 98, 99, 102, 103, 104, 115, 119, 121, 122, 140, 157, 161, 162, 164, 175, 179, 181, 182, 186, 189, 191, 195, 202, 203

European Union, 13, 47, 96, 97, 102, 104, 115, 119, 120, 121, 122, 129, 157, 162, 191

Euro-zone, 102, 107

evacuation insurance, 174, 175

About the Author

Rick Todd is the author of this book and forthcoming books related to finance, travel and overseas living. He is an American who lived abroad for four years in three different countries, including the United Kingdom, the United Arab Emirates (specifically the Emirate of Dubai), and the Kingdom of Bahrain. He is a graduate of Loyola Law School in Los Angeles, and Boston University. He specializes in writing and communications on financial services topics and currently works in the area of public relations. He is an avid traveler and has traveled to more than twenty different nations (and counting). He writes a blog at the site **Expat Investing** which can be found at www.expatinvesting.org.

CPSIA information can be obtained at www.ICGtesting.com
Printed in the USA
LVOW070748110313

323531LV00002B/267/P

9 781450 735605